The Mexican Kickapoo
Indians

by
ROBERT E. RITZENTHALER
and
FREDERICK A. PETERSON

GREENWOOD PRESS, PUBLISHERS
WESTPORT, CONNECTICUT

Originally published in 1956
by order of the Board of Trustees,
Milwaukee Public Museum, Milwaukee, Wisconsin

Reprinted with the permission
of the Milwaukee Public Museum

First Greenwood Reprinting 1970

Library of Congress Catalogue Card Number 75-111398

SBN 8371-4629-1

Printed in the United States of America

MILWAUKEE PUBLIC MUSEUM
PUBLICATIONS IN ANTHROPOLOGY

NUMBER 2

The Mexican Kickapoo Indians

by
ROBERT E. RITZENTHALER
and
FREDERICK A. PETERSON

The Mexican Kickapoo Indians

TABLE OF CONTENTS

Illustrations

The Mexican Kickapoo Indians

PREFACE

This report is of a preliminary nature due to the shortness of time actually spent in the field. We lived in the Kickapoo village for two weeks, spending a third week in the vicinity interviewing both Kickapoo and non-Kickapoo. Fortunately, we were able to make full use of our time, and accomplished, we believe, a tremendous amount under the circumstances. The excellent command of Spanish of one of the authors made communication the best possible without actually working in Algonkian. We had no difficulty in finding ready informants, but also encountered curt refusal and extreme suspicion among some of the older men contacted. We used no women informants, mostly because we found none who spoke more than fragmentary Spanish. The men were completely secretive about religious life, and it was impossible to obtain any really adequate information on this subject; such information as we did secure was mainly from non-Kickapoo. Although we made many friends, and visitors to our wigwam were common almost to the point of distraction, we were constantly being asked by informants, or stopped by strangers on the street and quizzed as to what we were doing in the village, sometimes in a surly tone.

When we had been in the village for ten days, we were summoned to a council meeting consisting of 34 men who barely listened to our case and then informed us that we would have to leave. We had secured permission to work from the civil chief upon our arrival, and the decision of the council came as a bombshell. We asked, and received, four days of grace to complete our collection of ethnographic specimens, and continued our work with informants during this period. We considered petitioning the leaders for permission to return after the New Year's ceremony, but decided that it would be in the best interests of future field workers not to chance a possible altercation, and to concur in the council's order. The reasons for our expulsion are as follows:

1. The conservative group now in control just did not want any foreigners staying in the village.

2. We had been told to obtain the permission of the civil chief who is recognized as the Kickapoo leader by the Mexican Government. However, we discovered that there were two rival factions, but by that time it was too late to begin explanation to, and placation of the second group.

3. Our arrival was ill-timed. The village was in preparation for the big religious event of the year, to take place in several weeks and which no whites or Mexicans are allowed to attend. The religious chief was largely responsible for our expulsion.

Our field stay, however, was a rich and exciting experience with some traumatic moments involved. It was with reluctance that we left this ethnographer's paradise. On the credit side of the ledger was the securing of valuable field notes both by interview and observation, a fine representative collection of specimens, and about 100 black-and-white photographs and 1100 feet of kodachrome motion pictures. Photographically, the village was a three-ring circus, and it was heart-breaking for a photographer to leave, particularly in view of the fact that the religious games, such as lacrosse and the woman's ball game, were soon to begin.

It is the hope of the authors that this report will be of aid to future workers in this field, serving to guide them in the process of entering and working. Had more information on the situation been available to us, we are sure that we could have established rapport with permission to carry on a full field project.

The project was sponsored by the Milwaukee Public Museum, with the approval of the Mexican Instituto Nacional de Anthropologia y Historia. Our thanks are also due to Mr. and Mrs. David McKellar of Eagle Pass, Texas; and Dr. Jacobo Chappa Long and Mr. Enrique Galan Long of Muzquiz, Coahila, who gave us valuable assistance.

PHONETIC KEY

Vowels:

i in feet

i in bit

e in make

ε in bet

a in rod

o in rope

u in room

ə in but

Consonants:

š in shot

ž in gendarme

č in child

g in girl

th in thing

Other consonants as

in English.

Signs:

′ accent

• length mark

au diphthong

INTRODUCTION

The Mexican Kickapoo Indians comprise without doubt the best preserved island of Woodland culture extant. The Fox and the Oklahoma Kickapoo have a well deserved reputation for cultural conservatism, but neither can match this Mexican band which has retained its central Alkonkian tradition to an almost unbelievable degree. The odyssey of the Kickapoo to Oklahoma from Wisconsin (where they were first contacted by whites) and their hundred-year stay in Mexico have, of course, resulted in some change, but such inroads have been of a superficial nature leaving the character and flavor of the traditional culture intact.

Even in terms of material culture, ordinarily the first facet of culture to be affected by a contact situation, the Mexican Kickapoo remain surprisingly Woodland. For example, upon entering this anachronistic village one is impressed by the fact that the people, without exception, are living in mat-covered Woodland wigwams (during the winter), and that public buildings such as schools, churches, or community halls are absent. The only non-Woodland structures to be seen are several Mexican-built pole storage huts. Even the village store, operated by a Mexican, is converted from a Kickapoo cook hut and is indistinguishable from the others except for its interior. Modern conveniences such as electricity, wells or running water, toilets or even outhouses, stoves, beds, or cots are non-existent. Some modern influences, however, are readily apparent as in clothing, kerosene lamps, flashlights, a few battery radios, barbed-wire fencing, and metal cooking utensils; but the general effect is one of entering a Wisconsin Woodland village of two hundred years ago.

Much more convincing evidence of their cultural conservatism than is overtly apparent, however, is to be found in their covert culture, the beliefs and customs which have been surprisingly little affected by three hundred years of contact. Here, then, is a going, operative Woodland culture that has undergone peripheral changes, but with the core intact. Such changes as have occurred have resulted both from acculturational experiences, and from an adaptation to a new ecological situation, and these will be discussed later.

How, then, has this band been able to maintain a vigorous traditional culture while the Woodland tribes of the United States have become considerably acculturated, some to the point of completion? The reasons most plausibly explaining this phenomenon seem to be:

1. Their own determined, almost fanatical will and effort to keep out foreign influences.

2. A non-interference policy on the part of the Mexican Government.

3. Their relative geographical isolation.

These three points will be discussed in detail.

1. Their own determined, almost fanatical will and effort to keep out foreign influence. This conservative attitude was apparent while the band was still in Oklahoma. One faction, referred to in the literature (U. S. Senate, 1908) as the "Kicking Kickapoo," began protesting against the inroads of white influence during the 1840's, exhibiting particular concern over the prospect of sending their children to school. The drastic action taken to retain their cultural integrity, that of leaving their homes and many of their friends and relatives to move to Mexico, was indicative of their state of mind. Once in Mexico a number of events show that this attitude prevailed. Persistent wooing by the United States Government to induce them to return to the States was ignored, and even a removal attempt by force, in the form of Colonel Mackenzie's raid of 1873, only dislodged them temporarily.

Their existence as a tight in-group, suspicious of foreigners and foreign ideas, is apparent in their negative attitude toward missionaries of any sect. Even Father Andres, a Catholic priest working in Muzquiz who testified on their behalf around the turn of the last century, and who was considered a friend by the Kickapoo, had no success in missionizing them. This is the only group of North American Indians to our knowledge that has completely resisted missionary effort.

Another prime example of their rejection policy has been their resistance to modern education. The local Mexican municipal government, deciding that the Kickapoo should have the advantages of modern education, established a school in the village around 1903 staffed with one teacher. The Kickapoo promptly burned it down and sent protests to the Mexican authorities. In the early 1930's another school was set up, only to suffer the same fate. Since then no attempt has been made to provide schooling for the Kickapoo. The tribal leaders are well aware that, once their children are exposed to modern education, the Kickapoo beliefs and customs will be threatened.

Another example of their rejection of the white man's world is illustrated in the case of a hospital built for them in the nearby town of Nacimiento about fifteen years ago. A main purpose of the government was the inclusion of an oculist on the staff to combat trachoma, reported to have a high incidence among the Kickapoo at that time. The Indians, however, would not utilize the hospital, so the staff was pulled out and the building now serves as a school for the children of this negro town. Some breaks in the armor are apparent, however, for within the last few years a few of the people have been going to the doctor in Muzquiz for treatment.

The Mexican Kickapoo have also been successful in keeping out the Peyote religion, even though they are near to a good source of the "button," and although there is considerable cross-visiting with the Oklahoma band where a Peyote cult exists.

A final, minor, rather personal example of their rejection policy was their ejection of the authors of this publication, not because of any incident, but just on general principles.

The will to maintain Kickapoo culture is based on a considerable pride in it, and a firm belief in its rightness. This attitude is reinforced by divine sanction. They believe that God either gave or taught to the Kickapoo everything that they possess or know, and it seems apparent that as long as their belief in their religion survives, their belief in the rightness of other aspects of their culture will survive. There is considerable of the "Chosen People" philosophy in their thinking, and among some individuals we encountered an almost arrogant conviction as to the superiority not only of Kickapoo culture, but also of the physical superiority of the Kickapoo. The latter aspect would be expressed to us at the end of a description of a lacrosse game or hunting expedition by the phrase, "But of course, you white men couldn't do that." This belief, then, in themselves and in their culture, and their relentless desire to maintain it by the exclusion of outside influences, is really the chief reason for their success in preserving their traditions.

A lesser factor which encourages a conservative policy is that of placing the control of tribal affairs, now as in the past, completely in the hands of the older men. While there is a "progressive" element among the younger people at the present time, their voice is a faint one and the decisions of the tribe are in the hands of the old. It would seem that all cultures are gerontocratic to a greater or lesser degree, and the Kickapoo are inclined to the greater.

2. A non-interference policy on the part of the Mexican Government. While the Mexican Government has altruistically intervened a number of times in the affairs of the Kickapoo, its basic policy has been one of hands-off. Its lack of success, particularly in the case of the school and hospital programs, has perhaps reinforced this basic attitude. The Indians have made their attitude clear. For example, during the visit of President Cardenas to the Kickapoo village, Papequeno, the chief, told Cardenas, "I am the head of my people; you are the head of yours. I don't interfere with you; you don't interfere with me."

The Mexican police do not patrol the village and will intervene only at the request of the chief, or upon complaint by a rancher that the Indians have been poaching on his land. The chief only calls in the police when serious difficulties arise. In the case of a murder, for example, the criminal is handed over to the Mexican authorities for prosecution and punishment. Such interventions are rare.

Besides the hospital and school attempts, there have been a few welfare interventions. During the Cardenas regime, the following items were presented to the Kickapoo: 28 mules (with harnesses), 14 iron plows, 6 wooden plows, 7,500 kilos of wheat, 2 harrows, 6 trowels, 4 sewing machines, 3 rifles, 150 pairs of pants, 7 bolts of cloth, 50 pairs of huaraches (sandals), 3 stallions, 6 leather jackets, and a saddle. In addition, agricultural aid was given and a successful wheat-raising program instituted. Such welfare interventions seem to have been essentially limited to the Cardenas regime.

There has also been some contact between the Mexican Government and the Kickapoo in regard to land problems, but in general the Government has allowed them to operate as a sovereign nation, and this non-interference policy has signally contributed to the Kickapoo's success in retaining their culture. It is improbable that the Kickapoo could have maintained such control over their destiny had they remained in the United States.

3. Their relative geographical isolation. A third factor of importance favoring the Kickapoo struggle to maintain their culture has been their geographical position. Their reservation is in a thinly populated area with an uninhabited mountain region on their west flank, and a 75,000-acre ranch on their northern boundary. The only settlement within a 25-mile radius is the town of Nacimiento five miles away, inhabited by about 300 people, nearly all of negro or negro-Seminole blood, the descendants of slaves left behind when the Seminole returned to Oklahoma in 1859. The Kickapoo view these people with contempt and there is almost no interaction between the two communities.

The Kickapoo, however, are friendly to the Mexican farmers in the vicinity, and have even begun attending their fiestas in recent years. The nearest town of any size is Muzquiz, population 10,000, which is 25 miles away, where the Indians do nearly all of their trading. Muzquiz is off the tourist route, and the few tourists who do come either are not aware of the existence of the Kickapoo village, or have no desire to see it. In fact, any would-be visitors to the village are discouraged by sheer physical conditions. In the first place, it is almost impossible to find the village without a guide, and secondly, the road is a rough one. In wet weather it is impossible, and in good weather it takes two and one-half hours to cover the 25 miles. It is also possible to reach the village by a bus which makes a daily run from the village to Muzquiz and back. Unfortunately for the visitors, the bus remains overnight in the village and there are no facilities for overnight guests. The bus service, started by an Oklahoma Kickapoo living in the village, but since taken over by a Mexican, is the one real communication link between the village and the outside. It is put to considerable use by the Indians, none of whom owns an automobile. The bus also delivers mail to the village, but there is little of this. There are, of course, no telephones in the village. There is no doubt that had a main highway been directed through or near the village, some disrupting influences would have been felt, as is evident in the villages along the Pan-American Highway.

Cultural changes due to acculturation and the shift to a different environment. While the over-all reaction to Kickapoo culture is one of wonderment at the degree of Woodland culture that has been maintained, there have, of course, been modifications of the culture since their leaving Wisconsin some two hundred years ago. Even in Wisconsin they had felt the impact of the white man, and their involvement in the fur trade meant certain shifts in economic life and material culture. Some of these were ephemeral adaptations, such as the concentration on trapping and a certain economic dependence on the trading post. In things material, however, the effects were more permanent. The use of guns, steel traps, steel knives, glass beads, metal kettles and other utensils, liquor, and horses, to mention a few, represented adaptations that were to continue down to the present time.

It is difficult to determine what modifications of the culture occurred as a result of their migrations and settlements in Illinois, Missouri, Kansas, and Oklahoma, and their close association with such groups as the Shawnee, Delaware, and Seminole during this period, but it is probable that some effects were felt.

It is a relatively simple task to assess the results of their stay in Mexico. Surrounded by a sea of Mexican culture, the Kickapoo were bound to feel its influence, but their island was attacked by gentle waves lapping at the periphery rather than by a tidal wave engulfing their stronghold. One of the obvious results of this contact has been their taking over of Spanish as a secondary language, and most of the men can speak it, although few of the women know anything more than elementary phrases. Mexican songs may be heard in the village, sung especially by the younger element. Mexican money is the medium of exchange within as well as outside the village. Burros are a common sight, and straw sombreros are in occasional use by both men and women. Mexican foods or cookery have not been taken over, although the people eat in Mexican restaurants when in town. Craftwork has not been affected, except in the case of a type of plaited mat of sotol leaves which they probably learned to make in this area. It is probable that they have picked up some of their penchant for bargaining from their buying experiences in the area.

The total effects on the Kickapoo of approximately one hundred years in Mexico are exceedingly small. It is in the area of the overt culture that some influence can be noted, but the covert aspects seem preponderantly untouched. The social organization, religious life, and political life seem to have escaped unscathed. Again, this is largely due to their desire to remain apart, and their selectivity in allowing new elements to enter. Also, there has been little intermarriage with the Mexicans. When it has occurred, it has been a Mexican man marrying a Kickapoo woman and the family living in the Kickapoo village. In such cases, it is the man who adjusts to a new situation rather than the woman, and the acculturational effects of such marriages on the Kickapoo appear to have been slight. Such unions were frowned upon in the past, but there seems to be no real objection to them now and there are five Mexican men living with Kickapoo women at the present time. While the number and effects of mixed-marriages have been negligible in the past, a seemingly growing trend in this direction is bound to have acculturational impact on Kickapoo culture in the future.

Perhaps the most important acculturational effects within the last ten years result from the growing popularity of migratory labor expeditions to the United States. Due to a serious drought, which has lasted almost ten years and which has ruined much of the pasture lands and made agriculture all but impossible without irrigation, the Kickapoo have become wage earners for at least part of each year. In March, most of the able-bodied men and their families migrate to the States to harvest crops, not only in the Southwest, but as far east as Michigan and Wisconsin, and as far north as Idaho and Washington. The effects of such experiences are apparent especially on the younger folk, who have adopted modern clothing and hair styles, and, more important, new ideas and values. This is a big breach in the Kickapoo cultural fortress, and if the migratory-labor pattern persists, it is bound to have a growing and profound influence on Kickapoo culture.

Some interesting changes in Kickapoo culture have also resulted from their shift from a forest to a semi-desert ecological zone. In the process, there have been important shifts in the food quest with items like wild rice and maple sugar dropping out of the picture, and fishing becoming unimportant. Food gathering continues, but it means new techniques and new plants to be exploited, such as nopal cactus and wild chile. Hunting is probably as important as it ever was in the Woodland area because of the good hunting grounds in the vicinity.

Besides new foods, the adaptation to a new flora meant changes in the materia medica, and material products. Split sotol leaves replaced basswood bark as a binding element. Birch-bark, so important in the Woodland days, was replaced by basketry for containers, and the wigwam is completely covered with rush mats instead of the former combination of mats and birch-bark. The birch-bark canoe was eliminated and no replacement was necessary. Completely lost, also, were the items associated with ice and snow, such as snowshoes, the toboggan, the game of snowsnake, and ice fishing. In general, the picture is one of loss of items of material culture rather than change. The things that have survived, such as wooden ladles, mortars and pestles, deer calls, cradleboards, moccasins, and rush mats are readily spotted as characteristic Woodland types. Several craft items have been added, among them a type of plaited mat made of sotol, and basketry of the same material, but the rest of the craftwork is distinctively Woodland.

Historical Sketch

The Kickapoo are one of the more poorly documented tribes and a precise account of their history, particularly the early period and some of their subsequent migrations, is difficult to assemble. This was a group that, after removal to the Plains, began a complicated network of migrations, resettlements, split-ups, and in some cases reassociations that is hard to trace in the existing literature. However, aside from their vague beginnings, at least the main thread of their history and movements can be reconstructed with some accuracy, and will be summarized under three headings: The Midwest Phase, The Plains Phase, and the Mexican Phase.

THE MIDWEST PHASE

While not recorded as being in Wisconsin in 1634 by Nicolet, the first explorer of that area, the Kickapoo with their close cultural and linguistic affiliates, the Sauk and Fox, were noted as occupants of central Wisconsin some twenty years later. It is possible that they were there and not contacted by Nicolet, but it seems more probable that these groups were driven into the area by Iroquois pressure, arriving during the first half of the 17th century, and apparently moving in from the south along the south shore of Lake Michigan. The Kickapoo were reported by Allouez, in about 1667–70, as occupying an area near the portage of the Fox and Wisconsin rivers in south central Wisconsin, in what would now be Columbia County. They were not a large tribe, early estimates of their numbers ranging from 2000 to 3000. By 1720, they had also ranged into northern Illinois as far as the Illinois River, and they and the Mascoutens were described by Charlevoix (pp. 269–271) as the sole inhabitants of this and their southern Wisconsin territory.

With the destruction of the Illinois Confederacy by the combined efforts of the southern Wisconsin tribes, about 1765, the Kickapoo, Sauk, and Fox were awarded lands left vacated by the confederacy tribes, and left Wisconsin. Some of the Kickapoo settled around Peoria extending their range south to center around the Sagamon River, and became known as the "Prairie band," while another group split off moving eastward to settle on the Wabash and Vermillion rivers, where they became known as the "Vermillion band." Their fifty odd years of residence in Illinois saw the rise of Kenekuk, the famous Kickapoo prophet, and the War of 1812 in which the Kickapoo sided with the British. During this period also, one group voluntarily emigrated to Indian Territory.

After the war came the development of the removal policy under President Monroe (1817–1825) and his Secretary of War, John C. Calhoun. Designed to move all tribes west of the Mississippi River, this policy had almost immediate effect upon the destiny of the Kickapoo. On July 30, 1819, the Prairie band, and a month later the Vermillion band, signed treaties relinquishing their rights to 13,000,000 acres of land in the Illinois-Indiana area, and accepting a tract in southwestern Missouri. The movement of the Kickapoo to their new home began the same year, but difficulties arose as some of the Indians refused to leave. The removal was accomplished over the next four years, however, and by 1824 there were 2,200 Kickapoo living at their new home on the Osage River.*

THE PLAINS PHASE

In Missouri new problems arose. Difficulties with the Osage over hunting rights, and the moving in of white squatters on their sixty-mile-square territory, created almost daily incidents which influenced the Kickapoo, in 1831, to petition for a new reservation in Kansas. In 1832 this petition was granted, and in the following year they began moving to their new reserve, a tract of 1200 square miles near Fort Leavenworth in the northeastern corner of Kansas. This settlement has survived to modern times, with the United States Indian Bureau reporting a population of 343 in 1940, although the question has been raised as to how many of these are actually Potawatomi rather than Kickapoo. Indications are that not all moved to Kansas with Kenekuk in 1833, but that a group split off and settled in Texas.

Some in the Kansas band were successful farmers, while another segment preferred hunting. In 1837 a few hundred of the latter group set off on a hunting expedition to Texas, where they joined up with the other Kickapoo band, and never returned to Kansas. In 1838 there was a reported population in Kansas of 724.

The Kickapoo seem to have been in the area which became Texas for a considerable length of time. Around 1775 they were granted a concession of land by the King of Spain, Charles III, in exchange for their services in keeping out some of the marauding southern Plains tribes (Fabila, p. 25). In February, 1778, the Kickapoo chief was called to New Orleans and presented with a silver medal by the Spanish Viceroy in reward for this policing aid provided by the tribe (Fabila, p. 25). This medal is said to be still in the possession of the Mexican Kickapoo.

The Texas band established a permanent village on their land grant, and in 1824 had an estimated population of 800, which was augmented in 1837 by the arrival of several hundred from the Kansas band. Texas, after declaring its independence from Mexico in 1836, honored the Spanish land grants of the Kickapoo. However, trouble with Mexico was still brewing and Texas, fearful that the Kickapoo would side with Mexico in the event of further hostilities, finally, in 1839, forced them to leave. They entered Indian Territory settling in central Oklahoma along the Canadian River and adjacent to Friendly Creek. Around 1858, they were joined by a group of the Kansas band under the leadership of the prophet Kenekuk.

It should be noted that the main contacts and associations of the Kickapoo during their Plains phase were with other Woodland tribes, especially the

---

* Most of the information concerning the Kickapoo's Illinois and Plains residence is derived from Grant Foreman's Last Trek of the Indians, based on Reports of the Commissioner of Indian Affairs.

Potawatomi and Shawnee, and their culture was and is almost totally unaffected by Plains culture.

THE MEXICAN PHASE

In 1850, a delegation of Oklahoma Kickapoo and Seminole, under the leadership of the Seminole chief, Wild Cat, journeyed to Mexico City to petition for land in that country. An audience with President Herrera resulted in their being granted a section for colonization in return for their promise to aid in checking the Indian raids along the border.

An agreement was signed by the Inspector of Colonies on June 27, 1850, in which the tribes were given four sites of land near Morelos, Coahuila, equal to those which the government usually gave for military colonies, to be held in perpetuity. Wild Cat was named as chief of the combined tribes, and he promised to make his people keep the peace and respect the Mexican authorities. The Indians were to fight the enemies of Mexico and especially to prevent incursions of the Comanche, Lipan, and other raiding tribes. They were to deliver all loot captured to the nearest authorities. They were given some tools with which to build a village, and a small daily food subsidy. According to this treaty, Wild Cat and all tribes with him were to renounce all salaries or subsidies from the United States as they were considered Mexican citizens from that moment on, with all rights and privileges.

The delegation returned and assembled a group including Kickapoo, Seminole with their slaves, Biloxi, and Potawatomi, which left for Mexico and settled at La Navaja, near Morelos. The Seminole, finding these lands too dry for agriculture, obtained a grant of land to the south at Nacimiento, near Muzquiz, and in 1852 moved to the new territory. They remained here until 1859 when they and the other immigrants were induced to return to Indian Territory by the United States. Twenty Kickapoo at Morelos remained behind, as did a group of about fifty of the Seminole slaves at Nacimiento. These negroes, choosing a free over a slave country, have maintained a continuous settlement down to present times, now numbering nearly 300 in their village some five miles east of the Kickapoo village.

The second, and more permanent migration of Kickapoo to Mexico took place in 1862 when a band of about 250, wishing to avoid involvement in the Civil War, and incensed by the Treaty of 1862 opening their country to a railroad, moved into northern Coahuila. In October, 1864, they appeared before the alcalde of Santa Rosa to ask permission to remain in that municipality until they could obtain a permanent place of residence from the president of the Republic (Mexican Committee of Investigation, p. 411). Permission was obtained, and in 1866 a municipality act formally granted them the lands at Nacimiento left vacant by the Seminole, and this has been their home ever since. After the expulsion of the French from Mexico, President Benito Juarez in 1857 confirmed the grant by the municipality. In 1919 the Kickapoo gained permanent possession of their lands by decree of President Carranza, at which time they were assigned over 7,000 hectares of land.

During their early stay in Mexico, the Kickapoo became involved in the complaints and problems over Indian tribes raiding horses and cattle along the border. It is apparent that, while the skirts of the Kickapoo were not completely clean, they never engaged in the large scale raiding current at the time. However, in 1866 a commissioner was appointed by the Mexican Government to reside with the tribe as a watchman of their conduct, to handle complaints against them, and to return any property that might be stolen. The Kickapoo leaders were warned of the serious consequences that would result from further depredations, and by 1868 complaints against the tribe had ceased. A commissioner was kept for their guidance until 1910 when the Revolution abolished the office, although since that time descendants of the original commissioner have acted ex officio in that capacity, with Enrique Galan Long of Muzquiz claiming the honor at this writing.

Besides the action of the Mexican Government, the border raids of the Indians led to an attempt by the United States to collect the roving bands, expatriate groups like the Kickapoo, and locate them in Indian Territory. In 1870, Congress appropriated $25,000 for this purpose, and in 1871 a delegation visited the Kickapoo to urge them to return to the United States, but met with refusal. In 1873 came the famous "Mackenzie raid" in which Colonel Ronald Mackenzie, disregarding international law, led a United States cavalry detachment across the Rio Grande and down to the Kickapoo village where he shot resisting Indians and took captives, mostly women and children, to San Antonio, Texas. A good many of the men had been away on a hunting expedition, and when they returned and discovered what had happened, they went to San Antonio to join their families. At about this same time a commission authorized by the Bureau of Indian Affairs arrived with the object of bringing the Potawatomi and Kickapoo back to Kansas (Foreman, p. 211). Their mission was successful to the extent of inducing all the Potawatomi and a large part of the Kickapoo to return to the United States. The Kickapoo were settled not in Kansas, however, but west of the Sauk and Fox agency on The Deep Fork in Oklahoma. The rest of the Kickapoo, numbering about 280, remained in Coahuila (Foreman, p. 211).

Mexico has been friendly with and tolerant of the Kickapoo, pursuing a non-interference policy for the most part and allowing them to operate as an independent unit. They were visited by President Cardenas in 1936, and on July 20th, 1937, Cardenas signed a decree reiterating their rights as follows:

"1. That the Citizens Papi-kua-no and Mi-no-ni-na are recognized as chiefs of the Kickapoo tribe located on the lands known as 'El Nacimiento' in the municipality of Muzquiz, State of Coahuila, and that they are obliged to watch over the tranquillity and betterment of their tribe. 2. The tribe's consuetudinary hunting rights are recognized, and the Forestry Department and its agents in the zone of Muzquiz are to respect that right, and not impose restrictions or taxes. 3. The tribe is authorized to take advantage of their tree crops and all the produce from their walnut trees, without being charged anything for it, nor will any person not of the tribe be permitted to exploit their natural resources. 4. It is resolved to respect the decree of President Benito Juarez given to the tribe in 1857 and the tribe is to continue in possession and enjoyment of the same." (*Archivos, oficina de Colonizacion.*)

At this time, the President also expropriated some 10,000 acres of land from the La Mariposa ranch which adjoins the Kickapoo and gave it to them for cattle raising.

While bad times are upon them at present, due to a prolonged drought, it is apparent that the Kickapoo like their Mexican home and prefer to remain there. They have, however, kept in touch with the Oklahoma band through the years by considerable visiting back and forth, sometimes for purely social reasons and sometimes to participate in one another's ceremonies. There are some cases of intermarriage between the two bands and some instances of members of one band setting up residence on the other band's reservation. Facilitating contact between the two bands has been the unique privilege held by the Kickapoo of being able to pass back and forth across the international bridge at Eagle Pass with no credentials other than a copy of an antiquated document reading as follows:

"Fort Dearborn, September 28, 1832

"This is to certify that the families of the Kickapoo Indians, thirty seven in number are to be protected by all persons from any injury whatever, as they are under the protection of the United States and any person violating shall be punished accordingly.

Wm. Whittles
Mj 2nd Reg. Inft."

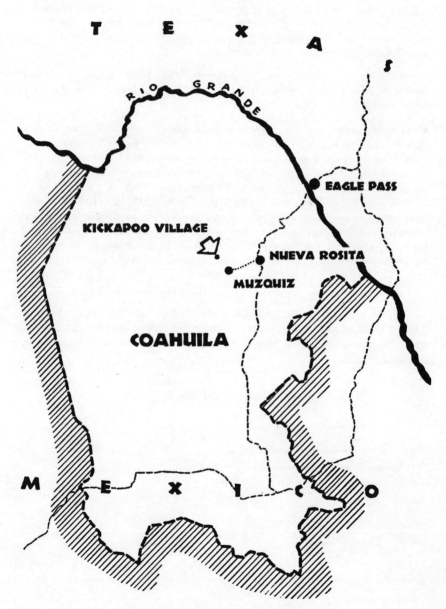

Fig. 1.   Map.   Location of the Mexican Kickapoo.

Part 1
The Modern Community

LOCATION

The Kickapoo settlement is located about 125 miles by road south of Eagle Pass, Texas, in the state of Coahuila, Mexico (Fig. 1). The nearest community of importance is Muzquiz, a town of about 10,000 inhabitants, situated 25 miles southeast of the Indian village. The village is referred to as El Nacimiento Rancheria, not to be confused with El Nacimiento Colony, a rather interesting town five miles away inhabited primarily by descendants of Seminole slaves of Negro and Negro-Indian blood.

The Kickapoo village (Fig. 2) is situated in the level Santa Rosa Valley, at the base of the eastern foothills of the Sierra Madre Oriental Mountains, about 1,500 feet above sea-level. The Sabinas River flows near the village and a number of springs give the name "El Nacimiento" to the region. This area falls in the Upper Sonoran Ecological Zone, with the most common vegetation including prickly pear, mesquite, chaparral, and sotol (Fig. 3). The average temperature during the day is 86 degrees.

SIZE AND POPULATION

The reservation consists of about 17,000 acres. The population is difficult for an outside observer to determine because of the migratory economic cycle of the people, but we were informed by one of the tribal officials that there are 62 families and a total population of 387 as of 1954. No tribal roll is kept.

CULTURAL AND LINGUISTIC AFFILIATIONS

The Kickapoo are most closely related to the Sauk and Fox, culturally and linguistically. These tribes were found living together in Wisconsin in the 18th century. They are also fairly closely related to such Wisconsin Woodland tribes as the Potawatomi, Chippewa, Ottawa, and Menomini.

Their language, a dialect of Algonkian, is still the primary language. However, many of the men are bi-lingual, with Spanish as the secondary language; and a very few speak some English. Few of the women speak anything but Kickapoo, and the Spanish of the men is of the vulgate variety. The system of syllabic writing in Indian, known as "babebibo," is found here. This is widespread among the Algonkians and must have been introduced in rather early historic times.

The Kickapoo resemble the other central Algonkians in physical type (Fig. 4). No measurements were taken but the men average about 5 feet 8 inches in height, and the women about 5 feet 4 inches. The men are of slender or medium build with good musculature and carriage. Corpulence is seemingly absent among the

Fig. 2. View of Village from Nearby Hill (MPM Neg. 35-17:21).

Fig. 3. Upper Sonoran Vegetation (MPM Neg. 500851).

men but is not uncommon among the women. Two distinctive facial types were noted, one dominated by a hawk-like nose, the other by a retrousse nose. Skin, eye, and hair color follow the usual Indian pattern, as does the straight hair and the prominent cheek bones. The Kickapoo seem to be surprisingly "pure." They do not intermarry with their Negro neighbors and there is little inter-mixture with the Mexicans.

PERSONAL CHARACTERISTICS

The Kickapoo are by no means a submissive, servile group. They conduct themselves with considerable pride both in their physical actions and poise, and in their somewhat superior attitude toward outsiders. We were constantly being informed that the Kickapoo can do things like playing lacrosse for four days straight. "But, of course, you white men could never do that." They hold the Negroes in particular contempt and there is a complete lack of interaction between the Kickapoo and the inhabitants of the Negro town of Nacimiento.

They exhibit considerable suspiciousness, especially in regard to outsiders, but also among themselves. We had to explain the purpose of a visit to an informant several times, and people would stop us in the village street and ask us what we were doing there. They are also great gossips, and a completely untrue rumor that we had a recording machine and were recording the voices

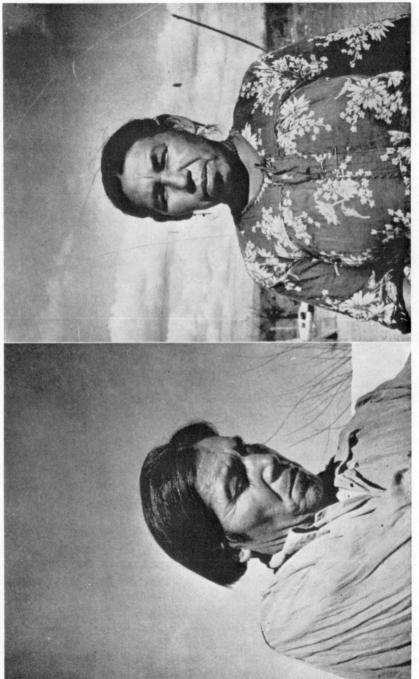

Fig. 4.   Physical Types (MPM Negs. 500874, 500882).

of the people spread through the village like wildfire, so that they were afraid to sing at night. They also seemed to do a lot of petty and grand quibbling and bickering among themselves, which is perhaps characteristic of small, inbred communities.

They exhibited considerable frankness and lack of inhibition. Our chief informant did not hesitate to tell one of the co-authors, who speaks excellent Spanish, to "come back after you improve your Spanish and we will talk," although the informant himself spoke miserable Spanish. They were unhesitant in coming into our wigwam, male and female, or children, at any time of day or night, for a visit, to borrow money, or just to stare at the unique artifacts of the white man. Their reputation for being liars and thieves was not borne out, especially the latter. In regard to lying, we did get some tall tales and it was necessary to cross-check informants, but little more so than in any usual field situation. They have a wonderful sense of humor, enjoying a joke at almost any time, and a high quality of humor is not essential in the provoking of laughter.

DRESS AND ORNAMENTATION

The usual dress of the men is modern working clothes (Fig. 5). Blue jeans or khaki work pants and cotton or drill shirts, with perhaps a wool jacket for warmth, are typical for village wear. If hats are worn, they are commonly of the Mexican straw sombrero variety, although for town wear, straight-brimmed felt Stetsons may be worn. Some of the younger men wear regular cowboy "ten-gallon" hats.

A few of the older men wear buckskin leggings over their pants (Fig. 6), and most of the middle-aged and older men wear regular Woodland-type moccasins, although in frequent instances a cowhide extra sole is added. Store-bought shoes of the high- or low-cut variety are common, particularly among the younger men, some of whom also may be seen in cowboy boots. For cattle herding, the men may don commercial cowboy chaps.

The more traditional Kickapoo costume is reserved for religious dances and games. The traditional costume of the man consists of buckskin moccasins, leggings, and loincloth. At the dances there is added a colorful long-sleeved "comanche shirt" made of sateen with paneled front, and gaily decorated with ribbon. Some of the older men still wear these shirts around the village, adding a modern vest and neckerchief with silver slide reminiscent of the United States western outfits and probably adopted by them during their stay in Oklahoma. A single eagle feather is worn at the back of the head on ceremonial occasions, or when they go on political missions, to impress the white man.

The hair is worn with a center part. It is allowed to grow long and thick, falling down the back to the base of the ears where it is clipped horizontally. A single thin braid, about three-eighths inch in diameter, descends from the back of the head (Fig. 7). This may be short, extending only to the base of the ears, or may be as much as two feet long. In either case, the end is wrapped with

Fig. 5. Everyday Dress of the Men (MPM Neg. 35-16:7).

Fig. 6. Older-style Dress (MPM Neg. 35-16:11).

Fig. 7. Hair Style Showing Pigtail (MPM Neg. 500860).

ribbon. Many of the young men have modern haircuts. Haircutting is now done by certain young men who have clippers and shears and are recognized as barbers.

The removal of facial hair is done with modern razors, by plucking with tweezers, or by means of a curtain-rod spring rubbed rapidly back and forth across the face (Fig. 8). We had to witness an actual demonstration of the latter method before we were convinced it would work. Native-made silver work is rarely worn by the men, except for neckerchief slides or earrings, worn in the pierced ear-lobes.

The women wear colorful cotton skirts and blouses or full dresses of solid color or gay prints (Fig. 9). A second skirt is usually worn beneath the outer garment. Most of the women, except for the young, wear moccasins, but bare-footedness is not uncommon. Hats are rarely seen, except for straw work-hats worn to protect them from the hot sun. Native-made silver jewelry is worn, especially by the younger women. Bracelets, rings, and earrings are common, being obtained either from the local silver-smiths or from the visiting Oklahoma silver-smiths.

The most common hair style is center part with a single thick braid down the back. Young girls have a top-knot of hair wrapped with a piece of ribbon, worn at the front-center. It is discarded at puberty, indicating that they are of marriageable age. A few "permanents" were noted among the younger set, and the use of lipstick was observed in several instances. Combs, including the native-made silver variety, may be worn at the back of the head.

THE VILLAGE

The village itself occupies an area of about one square mile. The 56 occupied houses are distributed, in a fairly even arrangement, along the roads and paths that network the village.

The Kickapoo compound consists of a cleared area, perhaps a hundred feet square, encircled by a barbed wire fence to control cattle. Within this area are found one, or sometimes two units consisting of a winter house, summer house with adjoining ramada, cook-house, and menstrual hut. Both the summer and winter house always have a single door which faces to the east. The elliptical

Fig. 8. Shaving with a Spring (MPM Neg. 500863).

Fig. 9. Everyday Dress of the Women (MPM Neg. 35-14:23).

winter house, occupied from October to March, is built like the Woodland
wigwam except for its covering of tule mats, rather than the usual cattail mats
and birchbark. It is of rather large size, averaging about 25 feet in length and
from 9 to 10 feet in height. The only openings are the door and smoke holes.
The summer house, occupied from March to October, is about 20 feet square
with 6-foot walls of vertically set sotol stems bound to a pole framework. The
roof is about 11 feet high at the rounded top portion, and when in use, is covered
by large tule mats transferred from the wigwam. Attached to the front wall of
the house is an open-sided ramada or shelter the same width as the summer
house and about 8 feet long. The combination cook and storage hut is similar
in construction to the summer house but considerably smaller. It is used for
cooking during the hot weather in summer and for storage of grains and meat.
The menstrual hut is an even smaller structure, either a pole framework covered with mats or canvas or a structure similar to the cook house except for size.

The village seems unique in its standardization of houses. All dwellings are
about the same in size and traditional shape, and there are no large community
structures of any kind. The only unusual buildings to be noted are the village
store (Fig. 10), converted from a cook hut, situated near the center of town,
and several Mexican-made rectangular structures of poles and cross-sticks.

The compound area is usually kept quite clean, being broom-swept at intervals.
Ashes from the fire are to be seen in a single pile along the fence, and a woodpile

Fig. 10. Village Store and Mexican Clerk (MPM Neg. 500897).

occupies one corner of the compound. Within the compound area, much of the work and play of the family takes place.

The hospitality pattern of the Kickapoo dictates that anyone who happens to be around at mealtime is automatically invited to partake of the meal. It is very common to see two or three guests at mealtime. A person can eat as many meals as he wishes at someone else's residence and no payment is ever requested.

Women are occupied with such projects as chopping wood (Fig. 11); the grinding of corn, coffee, or dried deer meat with wooden mortar and pestle (Fig. 12); mending clothing; and the great variety of craft work that women do. The men engage in the considerable visiting, chatting, and smoking that goes on in the compound; and occasionally may be seen engaged in some wood-working project, such as the making of a bow or ladle.

Along the roads of the village may be seen women with two galvanized buckets, engaged in their never ending chore of getting water at the river. Burros with loads of firewood are entering the village. Young men on horseback are driving herds of horses or cattle to pasture. People are going along the roads to the store to shop for a few staples, or to visit another household. Men leaving for, or returning from the hunt are seen frequently. Every family has one or two dogs which wander about the village. At the time of our stay, a considerable number of puppies were kept inside the houses for fattening purposes in preparation for the New Year Ceremony.

After dark, activity continues around the village. People are observed walking along the paths and roads carrying modern flashlights. Fires may be seen at the courtship rendezvous where the young people have gathered to talk, court, and sing. Considerable visiting goes on within the huts. Before retiring, the compound gate is closed to keep out cattle, the canvas flap is dropped over the entrance of the wigwam, and the interior slat-door is closed.

The neophyte finds it difficult to become accustomed to the night noises. These include the barking of dogs, braying of donkeys, cows lowing or chewing their cuds, the cackling of disturbed chickens, the beat of horses' hoofs, the courtship whistling, and the occasional raucous drunk.

Inside the house may be seen such activities as preparation of food, cooking, eating, sleeping, lounging, swinging the baby in the hammock, refueling and fanning the fire, sweeping the floor and sprinkling water on it, nursing a baby, sewing, carrying out ashes, and serving food from metal pots suspended by means of a chain from the ridgepole or standing on an iron tripod over the fire. The tripod (Fig. 13), purchased in Muzquiz, is of wrought iron and stands about five inches high with each arm of the triangular frame about a foot in length. It is a very functional piece of equipment, holding several pots and easily shiftable to take full advantage of the fire.

Fig. 11. Cutting Firewood (MPM Neg. 35-15:3).

Fig. 12. Grinding Corn (MPM Neg. 500871).

Fig. 13. Tripod Used in Cooking (MPM Neg. 35-17:10).

The house interior is arranged with a space on either side of the entrance for storage and preparation of food and for the placement of the water buckets and kerosene lamp. Around the periphery of the rest of the house is a mat-covered area for sitting, sleeping, and eating. This area is arranged in a U-shape leaving an open rectangle in the center for the fire. At the rear of the house, there are numerous metal steamer trunks for the storage of clothing, personal articles, secret paraphernalia, etc. In one house, that of the civil chief, 24 such trunks were noted. The women carry the trunk keys pinned to the front of their blouses. Small articles are stored around the walls of the house, being hung from, or wedged between the pole framework and the mats.

Kickapoo mealtime is at about eight, twelve, and six o'clock. There seems to be no variation in size or menu of the various daily meals, although breakfast seems to be lighter than the other two. The variety of the meal depends on the fortunes of the hunt, whether or not they have made a recent shopping trip to Muzquiz, and what the local store has available. Standard, however, at almost every meal, is a huge pancake-shaped piece of fried bread of either corn or wheat, wild game, vegetables such as tomatoes and onions, and coffee or tea. Other items of diet include a wide variety of game, fish, and fowl (including the domesticated chicken). Eggs are commonly eaten. Wild fruits and vegetables such as cherries, blackberries, strawberries, raspberries, grapes, prickly pear fruit, and mushrooms are gathered. Previous to the drought, fruit trees such as apple, peach, orange, lemon, and fig were grown and the fruit eaten and sold. Foods also popular with them, according to the local storekeeper, are soda crackers, sweet rolls, sardines, oranges, sweet potatoes, and squash.

The meals are served on enamel-ware dishes and cups either with a metal serving spoon or with one of the traditional large wooden spoons equipped with curved handle. The whole family with guests will squat or sit on the matted area at one side of the house and eat the meal together. No knives or forks are used in eating, although a knife is used to carve meats. A large metal serving spoon is the only eating utensil, and the fingers are in considerable use in conveying food to the mouth. A prayer may be offered before or after a meal, or both. There seem to be no food taboos, although such animals as the coyote, snake, and buzzard are never killed.

The Kickapoo sleep on the floor in winter and on sleeping platforms in the summer. On either floor or platform are laid several thicknesses of mats. The Kickapoo sleep in their undergarments between commercial blankets, and sometimes have homemade quilts to cover themselves. The use of sheets was not noted. We were told that newly married couples spent the first night on the north side of the house, but that afterwards, they could sleep either on the north or south side. Unmarried folk sleep toward the back of the house on the west side. Retiring time fluctuates considerably. The old folks go to bed between nine and eleven o'clock, but the adolescents stay up considerably later. This is looked on unfavorably by the older people.

The Kickapoo rise in the morning from around sunrise to about an hour after sunrise. The women rise first, stirring up the fire, chopping wood. When everything is ready for breakfast, the men also rise.

ECONOMIC LIFE

The most important economic pursuits at the present time are hunting and migratory labor in the western United States. A five-year drought has reduced agriculture to a trickle, seriously reduced the raising of livestock, and checked the cultivation of fruits and nuts such as figs, peaches, apples, walnuts, and pecans. Wheat, once an important crop, valued in 1943, for example, at 63,000 pesos (Fabila, p. 13), has been eliminated by the drought. Likewise, crops such as corn, beans, and squash, once quite important, can no longer be grown. The situation has become so serious that most of the people have been forced to seek jobs as migratory laborers in the United States. The raising of cattle, horses, mules, and burros, which had become a fairly important source of income, is a minor activity now with the pasture lands all but ruined by the drought and subsequent overgrazing of the few good lands remaining. However, some income is still derived from this source.

In March, and to a lesser extent in September, there is a general exodus across the border to locations where the people work as cotton pickers in Arizona and New Mexico; in sugar beet fields in Utah, Idaho, and Oregon; harvesting cherries and cucumbers in Wisconsin; gathering spinach and cotton in Texas, et al. Usually when they have saved enough money, or when the seasonal work ends, they return to their Mexican village where they can live quite economically on what they have earned. They are aided in this enterprise by their unique status of dual citizenship which requires no passports for border entry. As they pay no income or property tax, and since a house is always ready for them, or can readily be built, their major living expenses are restricted to those required for food and clothing.

These migratory labor experiences have had the heaviest acculturational impact on the tribe. The people, particularly the young, return from the United States with new ideas on dress, hairstyles, living habits, and acceptance of authority. The old folks lament this straying of the young from the traditional Kickapoo ways.

The Kickapoo never attempt to compete with Mexican labor in their own locale. Whether this is a matter of pride, or is due to economic reasons, was not determined.

Some income is derived from the leasing of oil lands in Oklahoma. About twenty of the Mexican Kickapoo have landholdings near Shawnee, Oklahoma, which are leased out as oil or farm lands, although the income is not over a few hundred dollars per person a year. There are no annuities or subsidies granted to the Kickapoo except in the case of the civil chief, Papikwano, who is given seventy-five pesos a month by the Mexican Government.

There are no really rich or poor in the village except for one enterprising Kickapoo, originally from Oklahoma. This individual, Oscar Zukwe, has accumulated a considerable herd of cattle, several trucks, has owned two busses which ran to Muzquiz, and is reputed to have considerable income from oil leases in Oklahoma. He is said also to have a very respectable amount of capital, which, according to a member of the family, amounts to two million pesos. Some of the people consider his local land manipulations and leasings unscrupulous, and this appears to have some foundation in fact.

Another minor source of income for the Kickapoo is derived from handicrafts. Moccasins and baskets are sold in the nearby towns, and there is also some market for tanned buckskin.

The traditionally important occupation, hunting, is still of both economic and ceremonial importance. While the man is in the Kickapoo village, his most important occupation remains that of hunting. Wild game is an important item of food, and to be a great hunter is one of the main goals of the Kickapoo. Game is still plentiful in the nearby hills and mountains. By far the most important animal hunted is the deer. Other animals of importance are bear, mountain lion, and *jabali* (peccary). Of lesser importance are muskrat, badger, rabbit, bobcat, fox, raccoon, wild turkey, pigeon, and partridge. In former days, the buffalo and the short-haired mountain goat were hunted, but they have been exterminated in this region.

The attitude of the Kickapoo toward the deer is well described by one of our informants. "The deer is considered to be the Indian's special food. There is none better. He is ours peculiarly. We never used to ask permission to go on property of the ranchers. The deer was put here for everyone. But laws were passed prohibiting us from doing this. But we still say to the ranchers, 'If you call the deer your property, where is your brand on him? You did not raise him. God raised him, and God has given him to us, and he is ours. So let's see your brand on him.'"

The attitude toward the deer is also shown by the chief's request to us to inform the President of the United States of the following: "That the President of the United States should order United States citizens to let the Kickapoo enter into their ranch lands bordering on Kickapoo territory, as the deer are sacred to the Kickapoo; that deer are our sustenance, our clothing, our basis for rituals, our offerings. Without deer, we will lose everything: our habits, customs, traditions, and ceremonies."

The manner in which the Kickapoo child has been conditioned to the hunt has already been discussed. By the time he has reached adolescence, he has acquired knowledge and skill sufficient for him to take his place in this phase of the economic life.

The bow and arrow is no longer used for hunting except by the younger boys. The young men and adults use the 30-30 Winchester rifle as the preferred weapon. They also use the 30-06, and occasionally a 10-gauge shotgun; while for birds, a 12-gauge shotgun may be used. Some of the Oklahoma Kickapoo have brought in 22's, but this is "new style" and is not looked upon with favor here.

Most of the hunting is done during the day, but "deer-shining" at night, with flashlights, is also practiced. In former days, a big hunt was held in the fall which would last for from two to three months. At such times, they would take the women and horses and move to the hunting grounds in mass. It is said that on one such hunt 1400 deer were killed. A leader was selected and prayers were offered so that no sickness or accident would occur, and so that they would have successful hunting. The leader was in complete charge of the hunt, responsible for decisions as to where to go and for assignment of stations for the deer drive. On the deer drive, men were stationed along peaks overlooking an arroyo. A lookout spotted the game, and beaters drove the animals down the arroyo where the hunters would dispatch them. At the present time, hunting is done mainly in groups of two or three, although they may be gone for long periods and range for several hundred miles, particularly to the west and south, covering the states of Nuevo Leon, Durango, Coahuila, and parts of the states of Tamulipas, Chihuahua, and Sonora.

Men usually hunt with certain partners, but only one man in the group is considered the leader. A two-piece wooden deer-call is used, particularly during July when the fawns are being born. The calls are blown to imitate the sound of a fawn in trouble. This will attract deer as well as other animals of prey who come to the scene in search of the fawn. When game is shot, the animal is skinned, cut up, and divided among the hunters. The person shooting the animal gets the hide and the tongue, while the meat is equally divided. The raw liver is usually eaten immediately. If the party is mounted, the meat is tied onto the saddle. If the party is afoot, the animal may be fastened to a pole and carried back to the village on the hunters' shoulders. When alone, a hunter will split open the deer, insert his head in the rib cage with the rest of the animal slung over his back, or carried on the back with the aid of a tump line across the chest, and carry it to the village. Upon return to the village, a prayer of thanks is offered for the successful hunt and safe return.

Deer tongues and ribs are used on ceremonial occasions, the latter being in much demand during the New Year's Ceremony.

Our inquiry as to whether or not the chief could impose hunting taboos, in times of the scarcity of certain animals, led to the following comment:

"You whites and Mexicans have studied such things. You think that game disappears. The Indian does not think in this fashion. God has put the deer, bear, Indian, and White on this world, all together, so that all of them should multiply. The animal helps man to live long. The only one to stop the animals, or exterminate them, is God himself. When he comes to finish the animal, he will finish with everything, man too. But as long as man, Indian and White, are here, animals will be here also. According to my beliefs this will always be so. I will always believe this. It is thus that I can never tell any of my people not to hunt. This is only the privilege of God."

Another interesting comment on conservation was given to us by another informant, as follows:

"If you white men hadn't come in here and blinded the deer, poisoned them, set traps for them, and shot them without needing them for food, there would still be plenty of them; enough for you and for the Indian. It was at the time that you were finishing off the game that you began to build zoos and museums to keep what was left. You are scared now that everything is going to be shot off, so you make laws now. But if you had been considerate and paid attention to natural laws of hunting, there would still be plenty today. You also came with the big shotguns, with big barrels and lots of shot. You knocked down seven, ten, maybe fifteen birds with one shot. This is terrible waste and extravagance. This is not obeying the laws of nature. If it were not for this, there would be plenty of birds today for all. You also poisoned the water-holes of buffalo, and killed thousands for sport. You only took their hides, for souvenirs, leaving all the meat behind to rot in the sun. If it would not be for this, there would still be plenty of meat today, for all of the Indians and for you."

Food or salt is never put out to attract the deer. It is said that hunting should be done at sunrise, noon, or sunset when the animals are active. An animal is never shot while lying down. There seem to have been no family or group hunting territories, and the absence of bear ceremonialism, as practiced among the Central Algonkians, was noted.

The only animals which are never killed are snakes, buzzards, and coyotes. It is said that the coyote signals the presence of game and so should not be killed, while snakes should not be killed because it would incur their enmity.

Trapping is much less extensive than hunting. Steel traps are used exclusively, although they still know how to make a type of box trap. Traps are used for muskrat, mink, badger, fox, raccoon, and peccary, and some birds such as quail. Traps are placed along the paths made by the animals or near where birds are known to perch. Corn was used as bait with the box traps but no bait is employed for the steel traps. For the larger animals, such as peccary, the trap is placed in a small hole and covered with a piece of paper over which dirt is strewn. Animals are trapped for food, and the skins are sold to provide another source of income.

Fishing is an unimportant source of food since the drought has dried up most of the rivers in the immediate vicinity. Expeditions must now be made to the larger rivers off the reservation.

Fishing techniques currently employed include use of the modern hook, line, and bait; bow and arrow; and spear. Special fishing arrows are made, usually of peach wood, with conical iron points and no fletching. These are considerably longer than the usual hunting arrow. Spearing is done with a four-foot wooden shaft tipped with a conical iron point. The fisherman will strip and swim or walk in the water in search of holes where the fish are hiding. The spear is thrust at the fish rather than thrown. No traps, weirs, or fish poisons are employed by the Kickapoo.

The gathering of wild foods augments the diet and income. Such things as berries, wild chile, prickly pear fruit, grapes, and cherries are examples.

PROPERTY

There are two types of property among the Kickapoo, personal and communal. Communal property consists of (1) the land and its natural resources, including flora, fauna, and minerals; and (2) agricultural implements. While all the land is held in common, each family has been provided with a parcel of land for its own use. Such a parcel is regarded as the full possession of the occupant as long as he or his descendants make use of it. Agricultural lands and pasture lands are also held in common, with the usufruct policy again employed.

Personal property consists largely of the products of a person's labor: such as raised or gathered produce, earned income, manufactured products such as craft articles, and improvements on the land such as the houses. Houses are the personal property of the women. Other property individually owned includes personal articles such as clothing, ornaments, tools, and weapons.

That the individual has practical jurisdiction over his assigned dwelling land was illustrated by the following example. When the council had informed us that we had to leave the village, the lady whose property we were renting became very indignant and told us that the council had no jurisdiction over her land, that we could stay there as long as we wanted to, and that no one could trespass without permission.

The trend in property rights seems to be moving toward individual rather than collective. A source of factionalism is evidenced in the two attitudes, one tending toward communal emphasis as represented by the older, conservative group, and the other agitating for more individual ownership and represented by the younger, more acculturated element.

There also seems to be a trend toward individual rather than communal effort, although public improvement such as road repair is still a communal effort. It is interesting to note that no public officer of the tribe receives any payment from the tribe for his official duties, such as chief, interpreter, grave watchmen, policemen, and town crier. The town crier was an interesting phenomenon of former times. A person chosen by the chief walked through the village shouting the latest news, announcements of meetings, and publicly reprimanding people against whom complaints of noise or disorderly conduct had been raised. These appear to correspond to the ceremonial runners described by Michelson and Jones for the Fox (Jones, p. 83; Michelson, p. 1-50). At present, announcements of meetings are carried by messengers going from house to house.

POLITICAL LIFE

The present nominal leader of the Kickapoo is a civil chief, named Papik-wano, who is 74 years old, as of 1954 (Fig. 14). He is recognized as chief by the Mexican Government and is given an annuity of 75 pesos a month. Chieftainship is hereditary through the male line, with the oldest son inheriting the post. If the chief has no son, and dies, the male members of the tribe get together and select a successor. However, a chief with no son can, on approaching death, name his own successor. If the son of the chief is too young to succeed the father, the council can name a temporary leader until the son attains the age when he can rule. The council today consists of all the adult males of the tribe. The civil chief is the leader of the tribe for about eight months of the year, but relinquishes the leadership to the religious chief starting sometime in December. The civil chief is considered as a sort of semi-divinity deriving his authority from God. This chief is now assisted by an interpreter-aide, a man 63 years of age named Pisakana.

One of the main duties of the civil chief is to call meetings of the tribe and preside when special problems arise. He also has the responsibility of assigning land to newcomers; for instance, those moving in from the Oklahoma band. He is also empowered to lease land to outsiders. Some lands are so leased at present, and the chief is strongly criticized for what is claimed to be misappropriations of funds. The chief also has considerable religious authority and officiates at some religious events. He judges and punishes minor crimes, such as disorderly conduct in the village, and rules on domestic difficulties. Serious

Fig. 14. Chief Papikwano (MPM Neg. 500875).

crimes, such as robbery or murder, are turned over to the Mexican municipal authorities by the chief. Moreover, the chief has called in military aid to solve political difficulties within the tribe.

In former days, a murderer or thief was tied to a cross-like frame and whipped until ten sticks were broken over him, each by a different one of a series of persons serving in turn. Similar punishment was meted out to small boys doing wrong, except that the sticks were small and thin. A drunken person might be tied up until sober to prevent him from doing damage to himself or others.

Up to 1948, the Kickapoo had their own police system, consisting of two officials with considerable authority. They were highly respected because their authority came from the civil chief and thus indirectly from their God. They patrolled the village with long rods to mete out punishment at their own discretion. Indian policemen were said to be interfering with the Mexican civil administration authority, so the Aleman administration, in about 1948, forced them to disband. This has led to serious relaxing of order in the village, especially in the control of drunkenness and the conduct of the younger element, a situation which is lamented by many. The Mexican policemen only go to the village upon request and thus there is no regular system of control. Prompt action is almost impossible because of the ride of two and one-half hours required to reach the village from Muzquiz.

For about four months of the year, beginning in December, the civil chief surrenders his authority to a religious priest, at present a blind man called Achimu. During this period, the priest is in charge of the affairs of the village which are centered about preparation for and execution of the big religious ceremony for the New Year occurring in February. This is followed by religious games which last for several months.

Beside the civil and religious chiefs, there was a war chief in former times, selected on the basis of personal qualifications and abilities, a brilliant war record being the essential quality. He was picked to lead the tribe only in the event of military crises or expeditions.

At present, there is a serious political factionalism in progress resulting partially from a younger, more "progressive" element critical of the conservative and traditional viewpoint of the civil chief. Another factor has been the establishment of a council set up by the Agrarian Department of the Mexican Government, with some authority over land problems. This authority has been used as a wedge to argue for further power in tribal matters. A third element of dissatisfaction has been raised by the Oklahoma contingent which demands more voice in tribal matters. The real and serious cleavage within the tribe, however, is between the first two factions described.

Thus far, the conservative element has been in control and has maintained to an almost incredible degree the traditional culture, attitudes, and viewpoint of the Kickapoo. Some splits in this armour are apparent, and more modern elements can be expected to penetrate the culture in the near future.

SOCIAL ORGANIZATION

In spite of certain factionalisms, the Kickapoo community functions as a tightly knit in-group. It has made a fetish of the attempt to keep out foreigners and foreign influence. The collective interest of the tribe is still the dominant theme. It is also a very in-bred community, with everyone being a close or distant relative of every other one, and the basic social unit of the tribe is the nuclear family.

There is no class or caste. Even the very few wealthy families of the tribe are essentially indistinguishable from the rest of the members. They live in the same type of house, wear the same type of clothing and, except for some material possessions, such as trucks and large herds of cattle, no outsider would recognize them as being any different from their fellows. Even though they have some knowledge and appreciation of modern culture, they prefer to live and operate within the Kickapoo framework. They seem tied to the community by kinship, and perhaps by certain economic advantages such as not being required to pay property or income taxes.

There are, of course, people who are regarded with more honor and respect than others. Prestige for the men is derived from religious knowledge, civil or political power, recognition as an excellent craftsman, or skill in the hunt. Women may be highly regarded for their craftsmanship and industriousness, or for a considerable knowledge regarding curative herbs. In former days, the shaman was a feared and respected member of the group but it is claimed that there are no operative shamans at this time. Wealth does not seem to be a factor in the prestige system. In fact, the wealthiest man in the community is also the most hated individual.

Besides the nuclear family, the group is organized on the basis of kinship, bundle societies, and moieties.

Kinship System

The Kickapoo have an Omaha type (Eggan, p. 4) of kinship system. It is similar to the Fox in terminology (except for dialectic differences) and in behavioral pattern. The kinship terms of reference are as follows:

nɛmɛso′ha ....grandfather (maternal or paternal)
nɛmàčihok′omɛtha ....grandmother (maternal or paternal)
nɛsi′thɛa ....mother's brother
nɛoɛ′kwitha ....father's sister
nɛki′ha ....mother's sister, mother's brother's daughter
nɛki′aha ....mother
no′tha ....father, father's brother
nɛ′kwitha ....son, brother's son
nɛta′thɛtha ....daughter, brother's daughter
nɛtotɛ′ma ....brother, sister
uthɛthɛ′ma ....older brother
anɛkwiutu′tɛmani .....younger brother

omithe'ma . . . . older sister
othime'ma . . . . younger sister
ni'wa . . . . wife
nenapama . . . . husband

Bundle Societies

It is questionable as to whether the term "clan" should be applied in the instance of the Kickapoo system. There are four sacred bundle societies, but at present they are not exogamous. It is possible that they were once part of a gens system which did regulate marriage, but none of our informants knew of it for either the present or the past. The four* societies are:

Inunuthuskwatha—Buffalo
Mesikatenoithota—Universe
Nenemikithota—Heaven
Kaysinenia—Flowering Cactus (?)

The function of these societies is strictly religious and each has its own ceremonies and sacred bundles. Each has a recognized leader and an assistant. Information was very difficult to secure on this subject and some of our informants even denied the existence of bundles. Information obtained from nearby non-Kickapoo residents, who claim to have seen them, indicated that these bundles consist of deerskin wrappings containing pipes, flutes, and beads. The main ceremonies of these societies occur in conjunction with the New Year's ceremony held in February, and involve the opening and renewal of the bundles.

Moieties

A moiety system exists, but it is a specialized one, functioning only in connection with the religious games, as is also true with the Fox Indians. No connection between moiety membership and bundle society membership exists. There is no evidence that the moiety ever regulated marriage. Each Kickapoo, both male and female, is a member of either the Black (oškoš) or the White (kisko) moiety. Membership is determined by the moiety of the namer. If the namer is a Black, the first-born will be a Black. If the wife is a White, she can give her moiety to the second-born. If, however, she is a Black, the second-born is also a Black.

RELIGIOUS LIFE

Religious information was very difficult to obtain. They guard their religious secrets with near fanaticism. Some of the older people refused to act as informants on any subject because they felt that religion would be involved in any matter we would discuss. After we had explained the purpose of our visit to one of the religious leaders, he stated that it would be impossible to study any phase of Kickapoo life without becoming involved in religion. He held out his hand and said that each aspect of Kickapoo life was like the fingers which are con-

---

* An Oklahoma informant gave us a list of 9 societies known for the Oklahoma band, as follows: Blackberry, Eagle, Bear, Wolf, Tree, Thunder, Turkey, Raccoon, and Coati (?).

nected to the hand, implying that Kickapoo culture is so integrated and so concerned with the religious theme that it is impossible to separate facets of culture into strictly unrelated categories. We considered this to be a very wise and well stated summary of the actual situation. White men are never permitted to watch the religious ceremonies, and this was the main rationale for their action in asking us to leave the village. Information on religion will be difficult for anyone to obtain for quite some time. Those who really know the religious views and activities refuse to speak on the subject, and the younger or fringe element lacks the knowledge. Our information was mainly secured from non-Kickapoo living nearby, and consequently is sketchy and not highly reliable. Some information was obtained from the Kickapoo, but it amounted only to bits and hints that had to be pieced together.

The Kickapoo believe in a supreme being called kičihia'ta who dwells in the sky and who is believed to have created the earth and all things on the earth. The Kickapoo believe that their God takes a special interest in them, and follows the every doings of each person. This is accomplished through the assistance of messengers of God, who are believed to inhabit the trees, rocks, clouds, sky, sun, and earth. The Kickapoo thus view the world with an animistic eye, believing that life and power exist in all things both organic and inorganic. According to one informant: "The earth is an individual; so are the rocks, the trees, the clouds, and the night. They are put here as witnesses for the behavior of man. The Spirit is watching man always through his witnesses or messengers. All of his actions are noticed."

The Kickapoo are tolerant toward other religions and are constantly pointing out that their God is the same as that of the Christian and other religions. They say that their religion and Christianity are very similar in teaching good conduct, such as the avoidance of theft, murder, lying, and dishonor. They point out, however, that while the Kickapoo practice their ethics, people of other religions, especially the Christians, often do not.

Fabila states (p. 86): "The Kickapoo religion is philosophical and leans to the stoic. That is to say these Indians have defined and built up their ethics so that they do not concern themselves with temporary sufferings and circumstances. This is illustrated in the terrible disease trachoma which attacks them and which they accept as being the result of powerful natural forces and the will of the great spirit. But this will pass as all things have a logical beginning and end. That which affects them materially and spiritually is nothing more than the will of the great spirit. This appears fatalistic but actually it is a result of their mystical approach and their particular logic."

They believe that as God made the Indians and all things that the Indians possess, all natural resources and products still belong to and are under the control of God. Thus the civil chief told us that he could not place a taboo on the hunting of deer because the deer were given by God and God only has the power to deprive them of this privilege. The Kickapoo believe that when their tribe becomes extinct, God will destroy the whole world by fire.

Religious life now is in the hands of priests, who are always older men. Priests are honored and respected for their religious knowledge and rapport with the spirit world. Nothing abnormal is noted in the peculiarities of the priests, although the present chief priest has been blind since youth.

Kickapoo religious life centers about a renewal ceremony and feast for the sacred bundles, popularly called "New Years" by the Kickapoo, which is held during the early part of February. The ceremonies last for about a week and include both a large outdoor affair and a series of rituals held in the seclusion of the individual houses. The time for the festivities to begin is announced by a specially appointed watchman who watches the skies for lightning and listens for thunder. When these phenomena occur, he fires his rifle to signal the arrival of the New Year. Preparations for this event are under way for several months. Hunters are busy collecting a store of deer ribs, which have a special significance in the ceremony, and young puppies are fattened on special diets within the wigwams. People are seen making new clothing for the event, and new objects such as wooden ladles and tule mats.

The ceremony itself is essentially a renewal ritual. It involves the welcoming-in of the new year, the kindling of the New Fire, and the refurbishing of the sacred bundles. Houses may again be repaired, and a new gaming season is inaugurated after the ceremonies have been completed. The New Year ceremony also serves to some extent as a social clearing-house, an important time for the consummation of such affairs as naming, adoption, and removal of mourning for those who have lost their relatives, so that the mourner may now exchange his ragged clothing for new garments and ornaments.

The first ceremonies of the New Year are held within the houses of those who have recently lost a relative. These ceremonies can be held in any house as every house is considered to be a temple. The priest will pray and talk to the soul of the dead person telling him it is time for him to leave the earth, and instructing him as to what he must do upon reaching their concept of heaven. It is probable that at this ceremony the sacred bundle is opened and renewed, and a person "adopted" or substituted to fill the place of the dead person. The adoption custom is apparently similar to that of other Woodland groups, such, for example, as described for the Fox (Tax, p. 2767). About a year after the death of a member of a family, it selects a person of the same sex and approximate age to replace the dead person. If the time falls at all close to the New Year ceremony, the time of the event will be advanced or delayed so that it can take place at that ceremony. The adoptee receives new clothing and gifts but must return a like amount of gifts to the family at a later date. While the adoptee is now considered a member of the new family, he does not actually change his residence.

Fabila states (p. 89) that the war triumphs of the departed are recalled at this ceremony. This mourning-for-the-dead ceremony also involves the use of rattles and sacred flutes which are said to be used for talking with the dead, the music considered to resemble the voice of the God.

In another special indoor ceremony, dedicated to success in hunting and the welfare of the tribe, only men are allowed to enter, but the women are permitted to sit just outside. Over the sacred fire hang two pots, one containing deer tongue and the other puppy dog. The priest offers a prayer of thanks to the God for success in the last hunt, and asks for further success in the hunt and for the general welfare of the tribe. At this time, he talks to the people exhorting them to be obedient, moral, and observant of the traditions of the tribe. Singing, with rattles, follows until the food is cooked. When the food is considered ready, an assistant priest dips a wooden ladle into the pot and offers the food to the chief priest by placing it in his mouth. This done, the rest of the priests partake, followed by the men participants and, finally, the women who are waiting outside. This food has a sacred quality and this ceremony is compared to the Christian sacrament. It is said that those who partake of this sacred meal have previously undergone fasting periods.

The large public ceremony following these indoor rituals is held in a cleared field at one edge of the village, and outsiders, if any, are permitted to watch. A huge elliptical dance ring is cleared, along the main axis of which are erected two sets of crossbars in line, one for the suspension of kettles for the sacred feast and the other for the hanging of new garments for the women dancers. Adjoining one end of the dance ring, a small arbor is constructed in front of which are stationed the five or six singers and a drummer. The water-drum used was formerly made of a hollow log, but at present it consists of a large kettle partially filled with water and equipped with a tightly stretched and bound buckskin head. At intervals the kettle is upended to allow the water to wet the hide, which is thus tightened. A straight stick is used for the drumstick.

The ceremony itself consists of several elements. One involves the kindling of the New Fire. Contradictory information as to the manner in which the New Fire is kindled was obtained. According to one version, the sacred fire is lit from the old one, and the old fire then allowed to die; according to the other, the New Fire is made either by means of "rubbing sticks together," with flint and steel, or by using the bow-drill. There is one sacred fire kept burning throughout the year which is not allowed to go out. This fire can be kept in any house and its location is supposed to be kept secret from outsiders. However, the civil chief informed us that the sacred fire is now burning in his house. Fabila (p. 93) states that if the sacred fire does go out, it is considered an evil omen and the entire tribe is greatly alarmed. They disappear into the mountains then to obtain new fire which has been produced by lightning striking a tree.

Ten new garments are hung up on poles for the dance for the dead. Ten women, led by a leader, participate in a dance which lasts all night. The beat of the water-drum, we were informed, can be heard in the town of Nacimiento, five miles away. Sometimes the men take over the dance, and sometimes there is an interchange with a pair of women teaming up to dance with a pair of men. Near the end of the dance, at dawn, they take the garments off the poles in the following manner. The leader, at the first circling of the dance ring, takes one garment off the pole. On the second circling, the second woman takes a garment from the pole, and so forth in rotation until all of the garments are gone. Before they leave they take down the poles, fill their small pots with any remaining food, and completely clear the dancing ground. Nothing must remain.

During the night a feast takes place which consists of sacred puppy dog and deer-ribs. The puppies are killed in a special way, with two men taking them down to the edge of the arroyo. A pole is placed across the neck of the puppy and a man stands on each end of the pole to asphyxiate it and break its neck. The puppy is then held in the fire until the hair is singed off, and taken to the river where it is cleaned and dressed; the intestines removed are left in the river.

After the mourning dance, and the mourner has been dressed in a new costume, he or she is free to remarry.

On such occasions, both men and women are decked out in their best dresses and ornaments, with new moccasins and leggings made for the occasion, and feathers in instances worn in the hair. The faces are painted with commercial dyes obtained in Muzquiz. The women apply the paint in round spots or half moons, while the men use stripes. There was one old Indian, known as "El Rayado" (The Striped One), who on all occasions wore green, red, and blue stripes horizontally on his cheeks.

One informant stated that he had never seen the use of masks in the New Year ceremony, but has seen one man with a wolf hide draped over his head and back, with the tail hanging between his legs. Also observed in connection with the New Year ceremony are the Coyote, Buffalo, Turkey, Pheasant, and war dances, although these could be performed at other times of the year, too. For the War Dance, participants carried bows and arrows, clubs, wore feathers, and painted themselves considerably. There used to be a tomahawk that was carried by an old man in the dance, but he died and his son has not deigned to use it.

Dances not held in connection with the New Year are the Green Corn Dance and other first-fruit ceremonies. In the Green Corn Dance, held in January when the first corn ripens, a priest will offer thanks to the God and the first corn will be eaten during the dance. After this, anyone can eat the corn. These ceremonies have been eliminated because of the drought which has ruined agriculture. A Buffalo Dance, said to be similar to the Sauk and Fox ceremony, is held in spring. The sacred buffalo bundle is used in connection with this dance. In former times, but within the memory of most informants, rain dances were held. If it rained while they danced, they would dance all the harder, taking off their moccasins and leggings and dancing vigorously in the pouring rain. They might keep this up for two or three nights in succession without resting. It is said that the restrictions on hunting deer off the reservation have caused the drought, so it is no use to dance for rain until deer become more plentiful.

The adoption ceremony is not necessarily held in connection with the New Year ceremony. It is also said to take place in the summer and lasts a single night. The iron-kettle water-drum is used, and food, blankets, and goods are hung from an outside pole. The person taking the place of the dead person is in charge of the dance, or, if he chooses to substitute a lacrosse game for the ceremony, he will act as captain.

Nothing resembling the Medicine Dance (*Midewiwin*), such as is practiced by the Algonkian tribes of Wisconsin, could be found. The only perceptible clues pointing to its former existence among the Kickapoo are the use of the water-drum and the adoption ceremony. In general, the religious ceremonial complex of the Kickapoo is very different from that of the present Wisconsin Algonkian tribes. There is no Dream Dance or Chief Dance, and the use of tobacco, of great ceremonial significance among the Wisconsin tribes, has almost no place among the Kickapoo.

An example of their religious conservatism has been their rejection of the peyote cult. Although peyote has a prominent place among the Oklahoma Kickapoo and there is considerable mobility between the two groups, the introduction of peyote among the Mexican group has been successfully stemmed. Likewise, Christianity has made no apparent inroads. A sympathetic and helpful Catholic priest, Father Andres of Muzquiz, who made many friends among them during the early part of the 20th century, was unsuccessful in introducing Christianity. No missionaries have ever been allowed to establish missions in the Kickapoo village, and there is no indication that migratory workers to the United States have been influenced by Christian contacts, except for two Kickapoo who reservedly showed us silver crosses. It is apparent that if they have any Christian tendencies, they are not allowed expression in the tribe.

GAMES

Games can be classified into four categories: religious, secular, modern, and children's.

Religious Games

Such games have been retained in full vigor. They are begun after the New Year ceremony and may continue on until the end of summer. They are, however, mainly concentrated in the period just following the New Year ceremony, and again during the summer months of June and July. These games are played in honor of the God and constitute a kind of offering to him. The game is an offering to the deity so that he will give the Indian good hunting, plentiful food, rain, good health, etc. These games are considered to be a special gift of the God to the Indian, and when they are played, it pleases the God. The games are sponsored by an individual, who subsidizes their cost, food being the main item. There is no particular order in which these games are played; rather, the order is dependent upon the desires of the individual. In all such games, they divide by moiety, with the Black opposing the White. The moiety rivalry exists only during the games, after which it is forgotten.

LACROSSE. One of the still important games is lacrosse. The game is played on a cleared level area in which the playing field is about 300 paces long. At either end of the field are the goals, each consisting of two poles set about seven feet apart. There are no set number of players but each side has an equal number, and a captain. It is said that as many as one hundred will participate. The game ideally is played for four days, but, apparently, it does not always last that long. One game, however, lasts all day and is continued the next day. Before the game begins, each player places his bet consisting of articles of clothing, livestock, and other valuables.

The players strip down to loin-cloths, leggings, and moccasins, and feathers can be worn on the head. All the area of the body not covered by garments has color applied to it; ashes are put on those from the White moiety, and charcoal or carbon on those from the Black. Each person has his own lacrosse stick of the traditional Woodland type with the small circular hoop, just large enough to contain the ball, at the end of a stick three and one-half feet long. The ball is made of hard stuffing with deerskin cover.

The men are stationed on the field and the game begun by the ball being tossed in the center of the field by a non-participant. A player picks up or catches the ball in his racquet and runs toward the opponent's goal. When he is intercepted by an opponent, he will toss the ball to a team member, the object being to move the ball until it can be thrown between the goal posts. The ball must never be touched by the hands. The game consists of four points. Betting is done on each point scored with the side scoring the point collecting the bet for that point. The game can get rough, noisy, and exciting. It is said that the players may become so excited during the game that they will play all day without food or drink.

WOMEN'S BALL GAME. The women's ball game is similar to lacrosse except for the fact that a different type of stick and ball is used. The same field and type of goal is used as in lacrosse. The ball consists of two oblong bags covered with buckskin and joined by a short thong. This double-ball is thrown by means of a straight stick and, as in lacrosse, the ball may not be touched with the hands. The setup of moiety teams and the betting are conducted as in lacrosse. The women's ball game, however, does not last all day, but is played in the late morning or during the afternoon, and the game is completed with six points rather than with four for lacrosse. The playing is said to be accompanied by much laughter, noise, and excitement.

MEN'S BALL GAME. Another religious game, played on the regular lacrosse field with the lacrosse ball, but not the racquets, is the men's ball game. The teams consist respectively of ten of the Black moiety and ten of the White. The ball is thrown up in the middle of the field. A player grabs it and runs with it towards the goal until intercepted by an opponent. Then he either passes the ball to a team-mate or he may be tackled by the opponent and wrestled to the ground until the ball is secured by someone. While it is a rough game, the players must never become angry. One point is scored for each goal and eight points constitute the game. Only clothing is wagered on this game, and the bets are hung on a pole at the field before the game. As in lacrosse, the players wear a minimum of costume, consisting for the most part of only loin-cloth and moccasins, but some may wear leggings.

DICE GAME. This is a woman's game played with a wooden bowl and nine dice carved out of cow bone. Seven of these are elliptical disks and two are carved figures. One side of the die is colored either red or black and the other side left the natural bone color. The game is usually played in the early evening, starting around five o'clock and lasting until dark. From ten to twelve women usually play this, and money is bet on the game. Each player will put from ten to twenty *centavos* in the pot and the first person who scores twelve points picks up the money. There is no singing or dancing with this game, but there is plenty of excitement. The women seat themselves on mats on the ground and one woman starts the game by placing the dice in the bowl, flipping the bowl to upset the dice, and counting score. The scoring combinations are as follows :

All of similar color except two.............. 1 point
All of similar color except one.............. 5 points
All of similar color except one figure.........11 points
All of similar color except two figures........12 points
All of similar color....................... 8 points

ARCHERY CONTEST. This is apparently a religious game in which the Black and the White moieties compete in skill with the bow and arrow. Targets are set up, usually about eighty yards apart, and the Blacks shoot in one direction and the Whites in the other. The team that hits the target the greater number of times is the winner.

Secular Games

THE MOCCASIN GAME. This is played by two groups of ten each, divided by moieties. The game is played with four moccasins and, at present, a commercial sleigh bell. A player on one side hides the bell under one of the moccasins, and a representative from the other side has to guess which moccasin it is under. When he thinks he knows where the bell is, he will flip over the moccasin with a stick or with his hand. If the bell is located on the first try, the side wins four points; if not, it loses four points. If the bell is not found on the second try, the guesser's side loses another four points; and on the third try, it loses one more point. When the bell is located, the sides reverse the procedure of hiding and locating the bell. Songs and drumming accompany the activity of the game, and it is said that much shouting, laughing, and horseplay goes on. Before turning over the moccasin, the guesser will study the face of the hider in a psychic probing to aid him in locating the bell. This is a gambling game, as are all Kickapoo games, and usually is restricted to the men, although in instances a woman of the same moiety may be invited to take the place of a player.

HOOP SHOOTING. This is played apparently by non-moiety teams of ten people each. The teams line up in opposing rows and a hoop, anywhere from

4 inches to 2 feet in diameter, is rolled between them. Members of one team shoot at the rolling hoop attempting to shoot through it. They may shoot individually or collectively, and from a standing position or while running parallel to the course of the hoop. The latter is a somewhat dangerous procedure, involving the possibility of hitting someone on the opposite side. The arrows are painted in special combinations of black, yellow, white, and green, for purposes of identification, and are tipped with the common conical iron points.

Modern Adult Games

Some card games are played by the Kickapoo. Poker is the favorite game, five-card draw being the usual variety. It is played for money not only among themselves but with whites and mestizos. It is said that losses to outsiders were considerable, particularly when the Kickapoo used to have their harvest money. The Kickapoos' irresistible love for games being what it is, they also play blackjack, monte, and pako. Playing cards are purchased, not made. A few people play checkers.

Children's Games

The individual play of the children consists mainly of doll play for the girls and bow-and-arrow shooting for the boys. Group games include: a modern type of tag game, foot race contests between the girls and boys, and a boys' game in which players in a circle attempt to grab three boys who must make four turns around the inside of the circle. A bow-and-arrow contest is held by boys after the New Year ceremony. A target stick is set in the ground in front of a tree or plank and the children shoot at it. If they hit it, they score two points. Six to ten points constitute a game.

SOCIAL PROBLEMS

Health

The Kickapoo certainly appear to be a healthy, physically well developed people. Their active outdoor life, coupled with a wholesome climate, contributes greatly toward their present state of health. The presence of a good water supply in the form of nearby springs has been exceedingly helpful. Such natural conditions have aided their cause, for it cannot be said that the Kickapoo are a cleanly, hygienic people. They do not wash their hands before meals, and bathing, especially among the men, is not frequent. The following information was obtained from Doctor Long, a physician practicing at Muzquiz. "Trachoma, once a serious problem, is almost non-existent at the present time, although conjunctivitis is fairly common in the mosquito season. Malaria used to be a problem, but since the drought, cases are rare. I have never seen a case of small-pox, tonsillitis, measles, or mental disease among them. There have been a few cases of para-typhoid. The real problem among them at present is tuberculosis, with about a ten-per-cent incidence. There is some venereal disease. It is only within the last few years that they have been coming in to Muzquiz for medical treatment, and this is mostly for fevers. Formerly, treatment was entirely by themselves. A hospital was established for them at the town of Nacimiento, five miles from the village, in the 1940's but the Indians would not use it, so the idea was abandoned and the building is now a school for the colored children."

The government has sent small-pox vaccination teams into the Kickapoo village every few years in recent times and there apparently has been no objection or resistance.

According to Fabila, other principal causes of mortality are: typhoid, dysentery, pneumonia, childbirth, malta fever, enteritis, senility, myo-carditis, cerebral hemorrhage, whooping cough, and homicide. His figures, obtained in 1940, give a mortality rate of 21 per thousand. This rather high rate is primarily the result of high infant mortality. His yearly figures are as follows:

Per Cent of Mortality	Age
32	Less than 1 year
13	1 to 4
2	5 to 9
2	10 to 14
4	15 to 19
18	20 to 39
11	40 to 59
18	Over 60

Their own methods of curing include the use of herbs and native medicine, blood-letting, the sweatbath, and magical techniques. Certain people in the village are recognized as having a knowledge of medically useful plants and herbs. Such persons acquire their knowledge from their parents. No money is paid to the herbalist but he or she is given gifts of clothing or other articles. It is said that money is never given to the herbalist because God made the world, the sickness, and the remedy. The cupping technique is used for blood-letting. The afflicted part is pierced with needles to draw the blood. Then a section of cow-horn is used with the large end placed over the wound and the small end sucked on. It is said that the blood comes out black. A deer nerve, chewed to about the consistency of gum, is held in the mouth and serves to plug up the small opening of the horn. The blood is carried out to an isolated spot so no one will step on it. A leaf-poultice is put over the wound. There are a few specialists in this technique, either male or female, but anyone can do it if he chooses.

For certain types of diseases, the sweatbath is employed. A small sweat lodge is built in an arroyo. Heated stones and water which has been boiled with cedar branches are placed inside. The sick man or men go inside clothed only in a loincloth, and the opening of the lodge is closed. The water is thrown on the hot rocks to produce steam. The sick person must blow hard upon the rocks "so that the sickness will leave him." This apparently promotes inhalation and exhalation of steam. After the steambath, the person is taken to the river and bathed. We were told that the steambath is seldom employed at present.

Magical causing and curing of illness is accomplished by the use of sympathetic magic. The shaman can use one's nail parings, hair, or anything the person has used to send sickness to that person. The cure is also magical, requiring that a more powerful shaman be called in for the cure. It is said that such shamanistic duels occurred in fairly recent times but that now "all those old men have died off."

The Kickapoo have their own methods for treating a rattlesnake bite, and one current method for treating scorpion bite is to put kerosene on it. A technique for reducing swelling is to make incision in the swollen part and tie on a rag containing moistened gunpowder.

Crime

Crime is an unimportant problem among the Kickapoo. Serious crime is rare within the village itself, and does not constitute a problem in the non-Kickapoo communities with which they interact. Homicide is rare, as is theft. During our stay in the village none of our valuables, although easily accessible, was touched.

The chief problem, both within the village and without, seems to be that of drunkenness. Considerable drinking was noted in the village, particularly by the men, although it seemed to be of the variety productive of noise rather than violence. In connection with the latter, however, we were told that a person violently drunk is tied up until sober to prevent damage to himself and others. Drinking is prevalent among both young and old but seems to be more so among the younger set. We were told that considerable drinking goes on at night during the New Year ceremony. Little wine is drunk, the Kickapoo preferring mescal, tequila, and whiskey. Mescal is the most common drink, chiefly because of its low price. Mescal can be had for as little as three pesos, or about 35 cents, a fifth. That they recognize drinking as a problem within the village is indicated by the fact that a council meeting was held during our stay to determine what could be done to reduce drinking, particularly by preventing Mexican merchants from bringing liquor into the village. Liquor is prohibited by law from being sold on reservation lands but can easily be obtained in the nearby town of Nacimiento, and in Muzquiz. There is no law against an Indian entering a tavern outside the reservation.

Education

The parents teach their children economic and craft skills and proper behavior, as has been previously described in the discussion of child training.

According to Fabila (p. 94), "The priest, wise men and elders, are accustomed to rise at dawn to announce the new day. Shortly thereafter they gather the children in a group, sometimes in the open fields, sometimes within the houses, to teach them religion, history, tradition, ethics, and good manners. The apt pupils are rewarded with grains of boiled corn, but the lazy and stupid are punished by having ashes put on their faces as is done with delinquent adults. The teacher covers his face with a mask of white skin to which a white beard is attached to give the symbolism of the divine personage." We saw none of this in the village during our stay, and it is probable that this is a seasonal occurrence in preparation for a religious event.

The present educational system is entirely adequate as long as the Kickapoo culture remains intact and the village lives as an isolate. Education, however, is becoming a social problem and will become increasingly more so, because the traditional education is not an adequate preparation for the outside world, and contacts with the outside are becoming considerable due to the growth of the migratory labor pattern. The older element has almost fanatically resisted the introduction of modern education into the village. As previously stated, two schools set up by the municipal government were burned down, and the Mexican Government was informed that modern education was unwanted, now or later. The conservative element sees with great clarity that modern education would be a wedge to disrupt the old traditional culture. They have a sensitive understanding that their culture is a highly integrated machine and that the change or elimination of one phase of it would have effects and repercussions throughout the whole. As long as this group remains in control, the problem of education coming in from the outside will be handled in the negative manner of the past. How long they will be able to prevent a modern school system from entering the village is a matter of conjecture, but it is apparent that such introduction will be a powerful force in sowing the seeds of destruction to traditional Kickapoo culture.

Recreation

The variety of religious and secular games and amusements offered by the culture is essentially sufficient for the middle-aged and older group. There is, however, some dissatisfaction among the younger set, particularly those who have lived elsewhere and have become interested in movies and other amusements offered by outer towns and cities. The statement is made, "There is nothing for the young folks to do here so they often get into trouble."

A great deal of visiting, talking, and cigarette smoking goes on in the village. Much excitement is evident when a Mexican wedding or other fiesta occurs in the vicinity, to which the Indians can go, listen to the music, and see the dance. Attending Mexican fiestas is said to be a fairly recent innovation among the Kickapoo, but it also is said that they now will stop a Mexican on the road and ask him when the next fiesta will take place.

Part 2

The Life Cycle

PREGNANCY TABOOS AND BIRTH

A pregnant woman is expected to eat less than usual, and for forty days before birth she does not eat meat. She does not drink cold water or go out in the rain. She must not look at a dead man, an insane person, or a cripple or the baby will be born dead, insane, or crippled. Near the end of her pregnancy, the woman does little or no work.

For giving birth, the woman retires to the bush where a vertical pole has been erected. Several women assist as midwives. The woman grasps the pole, kneels on the ground with legs spread apart and, as the baby is emerging, one of the women places her arms around the chest of the mother and moves her up and down to aid delivery. Clean rags are placed on the ground to catch the baby. The afterbirth is hidden in the bushes or hung on the pole. The cord is cut and tied and the child is bathed in warm water containing a medicinal herb. A thin belt of deerskin is bound around the woman for abdominal support. She then returns with the child to the menstrual hut where she remains for thirty days if the child is a boy, and for forty if it is a girl. The mother keeps count of the days by notching a stick, or the hoop of the cradle board.

Shortly after birth, the child is put on a padded cradleboard, made by the father or borrowed from a relative. The cradleboard (tĭkina′gan) is a rectangular board about 2 feet long and 8 inches wide, usually made of cottonwood, with a hickory hoop to protect the infant's head. If the infant is a girl the top of the hoop is rounded; if a boy, the top is straight. Several turns of cloth hold the infant on the board. If the infant is a boy, a hole is cut in the wrapper allowing the penis to project. There is no footbar on the Kickapoo cradle as is found in the usual Central Algonkian type. Instead, a buckskin thong from the top of the hoop to the foot of the board keeps the infant from slipping out. Toys and ornaments may be hung from the hoop of the cradleboard. On the hoop of every male infant's cradle is bound a miniature bow and arrow to show him his duty in later life, while the girl's hoop is hung with women's trappings, such as needles, silver ornaments, or tiny dresses.

For about six months, the child is kept on the cradleboard, which is put aside when the child begins to crawl. It may be taken from the board daily for changing or exercise. After about a month, when the navel is healed, the infant can be taken off the cradleboard for periods of sleeping in a hammock. The hammock is merely a blanket suspended in the house by two cords at either end. The baby's first pair of moccasins have tiny holes cut in the soles, as is the usual custom among the Central Algonkians. This is done so that, if the spirit of a dead man still wandering on earth invites the baby to come with him to the land of the dead, the baby can say, "I can't make the journey. I have holes in my moccasins."

The child is nursed for about the first nine months. If a wet nurse is needed, she must be a relative of the mother.

NAMING

The infant can be named shortly after birth, but naming usually takes place two or three months later. However, if the infant is born a few months before the New Year ceremony (held in February), the parents will wait to name it at the ceremony. It is said that if an unnamed baby should die, it would have difficulty getting into heaven. The parents select as a namer an old person "who knows about such things" (i.e., has religious knowledge) to be present at the naming feast, along with friends and relatives of the parents. The father can also be the namer. The namer selects two names, announces them to God and the people assembled, and offers prayers for the health and welfare of the baby. The father picks out a name which will be used as the child's name during its life; the other, the death name, is never used until after its death. The child can be given the same name as one of the parents. The child keeps its name throughout its life, although it is said that in former times a man could acquire a new name through deeds in war. A special relationship exists between the namer and the child thereafter, and the former is expected to bring presents to the child at various times, and has the privilege of raising it should the parents die.

The child's moiety is determined by the namer. If he is a Black, the child is a Black; if a White, the child is a White. However, if the mother is of a different moiety than the namer, she will give the second child born her moiety. At the present time nearly everyone has a Mexican surname as well as an Indian given name, and names like Gonzales, Valdez, and Rodriguez are common. The child inherits its father's Mexican surname.

CHILD CARE AND TRAINING

The care and training of children is primarily in the hands of the parents. However, the grandparents, eldest brother or sister, paternal aunts, and maternal uncles have some part in the care and disciplining of the children.

Children are treated indulgently, being allowed an almost incredible freedom. They are highly desired and treated with great fondness. A wigwam door is never barred to a child. They are rarely whipped, but scolding is sometimes necessary. The chief form of punishment of intentionally disobedient young children is to rub ashes on their cheeks and forehead, so that others in the village know that they have done wrong and should not be given food. It is said that when a child has ashes on its face, it acquires wisdom and understanding from God.

The Kickapoo child receives training for adulthood at an extremely early age. The boy is taught by the father the skills of the man with great emphasis

Fig. 15. Boys with Bows and Arrows (MPM Neg. 500861).

on hunting techniques, while the mother instructs the young girl in the many tasks allocated to the woman.

When the male child is old enough to walk, a small but functional set of bow and arrows is made for him by the father, and carried by the child even before he has the ability to shoot. Young boys are rarely seen around the village without their bows and arrows (Fig. 15). As they acquire the ability to use them, they spend many hours shooting at objects on the ground, or throwing a ball of nopal fiber to the ground or in the air and shooting at it. One of the favorite amusements at the village store is for someone to buy oranges and roll them as targets to be shot at by the young boys. The one whose arrow pierces the orange receives it as a prize. After continual misses, the children may be allowed to shoot at closer range, but the orange cannot be picked up until it is hit.

It is in these ways that the boy is taught the skills traditionally essential for attaining the primary goal of the Kickapoo man: that of being a good hunter, particularly of the deer, which has great economic and religious significance. When he acquires sufficient skill, the boy accompanies his father on the hunt and shoots at small game with his bow and arrow, while his father hunts with the rifle. At about the age of ten, he may be trained by his father to use a 30-30 rifle. For every first animal that the boy kills, a feast is held at which prayers are offered and the cooked animal distributed and eaten by the invited guests. This Feast of the First Kill is a widely spread practice among Woodland peoples.

Training of the girls also begins at an early age. The mother instructs the girl in the crafts and duties of the adult. Young girls are to be seen carrying water, gathering wood, and helping with mat-making and other crafts suitable to their age-abilities. For example, we noticed a girl, about seven years of age, with a burro equipped with two pack sacks and a small ax, riding out to the bush to gather wood. In another instance, we saw two girls of about ten splitting and trimming the tule rushes to be woven into mats for the wigwam. Both boys and girls are taught how to ride horses at an early age.

None of the Kickapoo children receives any formal education. The conservative members of the tribe do not want their children to go to school and learn "foreign customs." They believe that the education of their children is in the hands of their God, and that nothing further is needed. The child receives such knowledge by fasting. At the age of six or seven, ashes are put on the cheeks of the child who is sent out to fast for a half day at a time. Later this period is increased to a full day, and finally big fasts are held during which the youth may spend several days fasting and acquiring knowledge. The length of the fast is up to the individual. If one dreams good dreams, one will fast to see if they will be repeated. If a dream is repeated, that is what will happen to the dreamer. If one has a bad dream, the fasting will be stopped for the time being. We were told that a guardian spirit is not acquired through the fasting dream. Although fasting is common today, it is practiced much less than in former times, a fact which the old men lament.

COURTSHIP

In former days, the young man used the lover's flute in courting. He would go out in the hills or climb a tree and serenade his sweetheart until she joined him. Not only did each flute have a distinctive tone, but also each flutist had his own melodies; therefore, the girl could recognize the one serenading her. The use of the lover's flute disappeared with the introduction of the custom of courtship whistling, which began in about 1915.

One of the most unique and interesting practices in connection with the present day life cycle of the Kickapoo is that of courtship whistling. Each night during our stay in the village, the whistling could be heard from dusk to midnight, or even later. The whistling is done by young people of either sex. The two hands are cupped and air projected into the cavity so created by placing the lips against the knuckles of the thumbs, held vertically, and blowing (Fig. 16). Three fingers of the cupped right hand are placed so that the ends rest near the base of the index finger of the left hand. The fingers of the left hand control the aperture at the back of the hands, opening and closing it to control the tone.

This whistling is not serenading, but an actual means of communication based on the pitch, accent, and cadence of the Kickapoo language. As most people in the village understand the whistling system, the whistler has to be careful of what is said, or people will mock him or make fun of him. The usual pattern is for one or more young men to build a fire at one of the several popular rendezvous spots in or near the village. The young man will communicate with his girl friend by whistling, asking her to join him, and the girl will reply that

Fig. 16. Courtship Whistling (MPM Neg. 35-17:7).

she can or cannot join him. The messages sent consist of standard phrases such as: "Come on," "Wait a minute," "I'm coming," "What's keeping you?," "No," "I am thinking of you." The identity of the whistler is easily determined by his manner of whistling, just as a person is recognized by his speech mannerisms. Although the system is used primarily for courtship, married men sometimes communicate in this way with their wives, but never other women.

A boy can communicate with another boy, but it is a fairly limited practice. The real purpose, then, of this type of whistling is for communication for purposes of courtship among young people of opposite sex. At the rendezvous a group of from two to fifteen may gather to talk, sing Mexican songs, court, and occasionally drink. Some of the older folk object to this practice, particularly because the young people stay out so late. In former times young people of fifteen or sixteen years of age were sent to bed soon after supper, but now they stay out until midnight. Even some of the younger folks of from seven to eight will hang around the rendezvous spots with their older brothers, learning to whistle and staying out late, much to their parents' consternation.

The parents seem unable to control this process. It was once banned while the policemen were in control, up to about 1940, because it led to licentiousness. This was partially because Mexican youths, although not understanding the messages, were attracted to the source of the whistle and found the girls quite cooperative. Since then, however, the practice has been revived in full force. This whistling is called onowɛ'čikɛpi.

Older courtship practices are still to be found to some extent. A young man may watch the young girls as they go to the stream to get water. If he likes one he will meet her and talk with her each time she goes for water. If his attentions are welcomed and they decide to get married, she invites him to her house to talk to her parents. If the parents approve, the marriage takes place. In former days no premarital sex contact was permitted. Besides reciprocated affection, the qualities sought by the young man were that the girl be a good worker; a good cook; that she be honest, clean, and good humored; and that she should not be too heavy for a horse. The chief requisite for the man was that he be a good hunter, but other desired qualities were sobriety and integrity. Physical beauty seems to have been a rather unimportant requirement.

MARRIAGE

None of the marriages is formalized by civil or religious authorities. Marriage is accomplished by simple Indian custom, with parental approval being the only prerequisite. In former times, there was a meeting and exchange of presents between the girl's and the boy's relatives. The boy and girl are considered married when they move in with the boy's parents and begin living together. After a short stay at the house of the boy's parents (three to six months), they may go to live at the house of the girl's parents, or they may remain where they are. Usually when the second child is born, the couple will build a house of their own in the same compound in which they are staying.

Polygyny is sanctioned but a man must be able to support more than one wife. Our informants stated that there were no plural marriages at present but that there were in former times. Polyandry is not sanctioned.

There do not seem to be any marriage prohibitions other than that a man cannot marry close relatives: i.e. a man cannot marry his sister or first cousins. All of our informants insisted there were no other marriage restrictions, and we made it a point to ask about intermarriage with persons of similar "clan." Any such former restrictions have broken down, and this is also true of the Oklahoma band. Most of the Kickapoo marry fairly early in life. According to statistics compiled by Fabila (p. 45), the model age for a girl's first marriage is sixteen.

DIVORCE

Divorce is as easily accomplished as marriage. Grounds for divorce are nagging, jealousy, and adultery. If a couple is living with the boy's parents and the man wants a divorce, he will tell his wife to go home to her parents, or take her there himself. If they have their own house and the marriage goes bad, the man leaves the house. Reconciliation can be effected by the man asking the wife to return to the house. In case of divorce, grown-up boys may go with the father, but the smaller children and all girls always go with the woman. Although divorce is easily achieved, Kickapoo marriage is not a brittle institution and divorces are few. Some people have had two or three mates but this is usually due to the death of a spouse.

OLD AGE AND DEATH

The grandparents can go to live at the house of either a son or a daughter. They can change off from time to time if they wish, and often do. If an old person has no family to take care of him, there is a tribal fund which can be used for his upkeep. However, only a few are in this position. The duties of old age are mainly to take care of the children in the household: to feed, dress, wash, and look after them generally. Besides stirring up the fire and performing a few small household tasks, not too much else is expected of them. They have a part in the education and training of their grandchildren. The older men take a responsible position in the civil and religious affairs of the tribe. They represent the conservative element at present, in opposition to men of the younger generation who are more susceptible to contacts with the modern world. Currently, the older element is in complete power in directing the affairs of the tribe.

If a man dies in the morning, he is buried the same day. However, if he dies after midday, he is buried 24 hours later, and an all-night wake is held for him with singing by the priest and relatives. In either case, the body is kept in state in the house and relatives, friends, and the priest are invited. The priest announces the death of the person to God. The dead man is dressed up and dabs of red paint are put on his cheeks and instep. The body is then wrapped in a blanket and bound onto two poles, which are carried on the shoulders of the bearers. The body is then removed through a hole cut in the west end of the building. The west is the direction in which the dead must go, the east being reserved for the living. Only men are allowed to go to the graveyard. The body is taken to one of several family cemeteries, situated either in the village or on a nearby hill. At the graveyard, the deceased is taken off of the stretcher and put on a platform. A rectangular grave about four feet deep is dug with crowbar and shovel. This is lined with stone slabs which the men gather from the mountains. The body is lowered into the grave with the head to the east, so that when he is ready to begin his westward journey to heaven he will rise and be faced in the right direction.

The corpse is dressed in ordinary clothing for a journey. A large wooden ladle, with food in it, is put on its chest and water is also provided. Stone slabs are placed to form the roof of the vault, and the grave is filled in with dirt, rising above the ground in the form of a low mound. On top of this, branches and nopal cactus leaves are thrown.

In a second type of interment, less common than the stone vault, the corpse is placed in a hollow-log coffin. The log can be naturally or artificially hollowed out. It is cut in half lengthwise; the body is placed in one half, put into the grave, covered with earth. The stone vault method of burial is more usual because it is easier to do. The Oklahoma band use the log coffin, but not the stone-lined vault.

Usually no markers are used to identify the grave, but the relatives know who is buried in each one. However, in the case of a dead chief, a marking pole about four feet high is put up, with a white flag on it, so that their God will know that a "big chief" is buried there. There is a special watchman to inspect the cemeteries and make sure that everything is in order. If a cemetery needs cleaning, he may delegate someone else to go there and do the work.

The house of the dead person is abandoned and a circle of ashes is put around it so that the soul of the dead can not re-enter. The house is left standing until the New Year ceremony, at which time it is torn down.

A man who dies while on the hunt, or while away from the village for some other reason, is buried at the place where he died. Suicide is considered to be evil and a man who so dies is not given a funeral or other burial ceremonies. A hole may be hastily dug for him and the body thrown in, or the body may be left in the bushes for the animals to eat.

MOURNING

The closest relative of the person who has died must observe a period of mourning in which certain taboos are observed. The removal of mourning can take place a few months after the death of the person, but this is an expensive ceremony and the people usually wait until the New Year ceremony.

During the mourning period, the widow can not put on new clothing, comb her hair, or touch the head of a child. She is not allowed to repair the roof of her house. She must use a stick to scratch her head. The touching of the head of a child will result in illness or death to the child.

At the removal of mourning, there is a feast and prayers at which time the soul of the dead person is released to enter heaven. The relatives of a widow comb her hair, dress her in new clothing, and decorate her with ornaments. The widow is now freed of her mourning taboos, and after four days may marry again.

Part 3
Material Culture

The arts and crafts of the Central Algonkian peoples are generally considered unspectacular. Art concepts were not highly developed, and the craftwork shows practical, often clever use of native material, but rather simple artistic embellishments. Art was ordinarily employed in the application of design or other embellishment to a utilitarian product.

Woodland craftwork was based on the utilization of forest materials, particularly wood and bark. Woodworking was competently done and the products included cradleboards, ladles, bowls, flutes, drums, mortars and pestles, tanning tools, ricing implements, bows and arrows, deer calls, traps, fish lures, lacrosse sticks, snowshoes, toboggans, and sleds. In the white birch area birch-bark had many uses for such items as containers, canoes, house roofs, torches, and mnemonic aids. Cattails were used in the construction of mats for house sidings, bulrushes and cedar bark for floor mats, nettle fiber and buffalo hair (and later commercial yarn) for·bags and sashes. Perhaps the most skillful and artistic products of the Woodland peoples were the woven ones: mats, bags, and sashes. Buckskin was used for clothing, and decorated with porcupine quills and, later, glass beads and silk appliqué in either geometrical or floral designs. Objects of German silver were introduced by the French during the latter part of the eighteenth century, and it is probable that native silversmithing was begun in the early part of the nineteenth century.

Specialization, except for sex, did not exist, and craft guilds or hereditary crafts were unknown. While certain individuals would be recognized as being particularly adept at a certain craft, every man was expected to do the men's crafts, such as woodworking, and every woman was trained in women's crafts, such as weaving. An exception to this pattern is to be found in the introduced craft of silverworking which was limited to a small number of specialists.

The Mexican Kickapoo have retained their Woodland brand of material culture to a rather surprising degree. Some products, such as birch-bark containers, have been eliminated due to the lack of a satisfactory plant-material substitute in their new location, but what has remained is in keeping with their traditional arts and crafts. Designwise, they are most similar to other tribes of the southern division, such as the Sauk, Fox, and Prairie Potawatomi, rather than to northern-division tribes, such as Chippewa and Forest Potawatomi. Thus there is a concentration on geometrical designs as exemplified in their beadwork, in contrast to the free use of curvilinear patterns, particularly floral motifs, as found among tribes of the northern division. However, on larger surfaces, particularly clothing, floral patterns are not uncommon. In other respects the craft products of the two divisions are very similar.

The following analysis is based on items collected on the 1954 field trip to the Mexican Kickapoo.

Woodworking

Woodworking is the work of men. Tools at present include the axe, curve-bladed adze, and knife. We saw no evidence of the crooked knife so commonly employed among the Wisconsin Indians of today. The smoothing is done with pieces of broken glass used as scrapers.

LADLES. The example illustrated (Fig. 17) has a 7-inch handle with the spoon portion 6 inches in diameter and 1 inch deep. The handles are usually decoratively carved incorporating human, animal, or abstract forms, and ordinarily culminate in a hook so that the ladle can be hung from the lip of the pot. Ladles are used for stirring and serving food.

MORTAR AND PESTLE. These are still very much in use for grinding corn, dried venison, and coffee. The mortar is a partially hollowed-out log with exte-

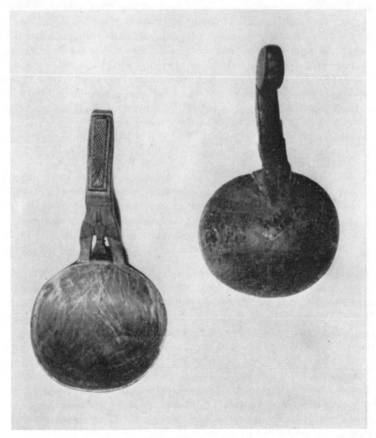

Fig. 17. Wooden Ladles (MPM Neg. 203815).

Fig. 18. Mortar and Pestle (MPM Neg. 203808).

rior shape expanded toward the top, but leaving a cylindrical base. The relatively small specimen pictured here (Fig. 18) is 11 inches high with the bowl 7½ inches in depth and 5 inches in largest diameter, but the usual height of the specimens we saw in use was about 2½ feet. The double-ended pestle shown is 32 inches in length. It is not unusual to see two women, each with a pestle, pounding in tandem while using a single mortar.

CRADLEBOARDS. The cradleboard is very much in use; in fact we had some difficulty in getting a specimen because the people who had them claimed either immediate or potential use for them. The one we finally obtained (Fig. 19) consisted of a hardwood board 7 inches wide, 2 feet long, and ½ inch thick. A hickory hoop 10 inches in height has sharpened ends mortised into a cross piece which extends across the back of the board. The hoop is given greater rigidity by the addition of buckskin thongs which are stretched from its top to the top and bottom of the board, and also by thongs attached to holes near the base of the hoop and extending from there to the sides of the board. The curved hoop on this speci-

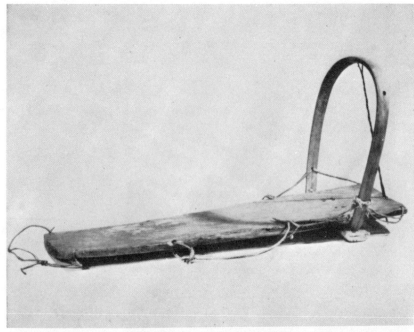

Fig. 19. Cradleboard (MPM Neg. 203805).

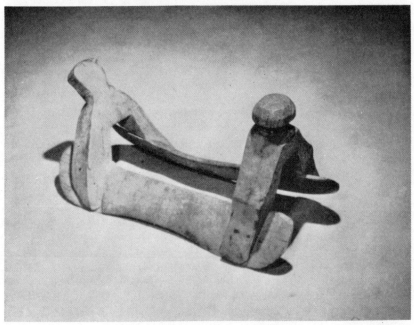

Fig. 20. Pack Saddle (MPM Neg. 203851).

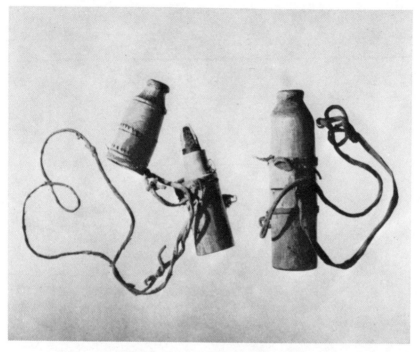

Fig. 21. Deer Calls (MPM Neg. 203809).

men indicates that this was the cradleboard of a girl; the boy's board has a
hoop with a straight top. Two thongs on the right edge of the board keep the
cloth wrappers from slipping up or down. A footbar, such as occurs on those
of the northern division, is not used on the Kickapoo cradleboard. Instead, the
thong from the top of the hoop to the base of the board keeps the infant from
sliding out.

SADDLES. While commercial leather saddles are very much in evidence, native-
made wooden pack saddles are also in considerable use. The specimen illustrated
(Fig. 20) represents the usual frame type, with ends consisting of four pieces
of hardwood held together with nails, and two parallel side bars thinned on the
outer side at each end to house the pommel and cantle. This specimen is 19½
inches long and 10 inches high. The few saddles we examined were of Woodland
western type, but none was covered with rawhide, or provided with rawhide seats.

DEER CALLS. These are made of two cylindrical sections of wood held together
by a fitted peg joint (Fig. 21). They are about 5 inches in length and 1½ inches
in diameter. The mouthpiece half usually is decorated with carved designs. The
mouthpiece section is hollow and fits into the peg of a second section, into which
a vibrating membrane of metal is set, resting on a wooden lip. It is said that
the deer call simulates the sound of a fawn in trouble, and attracts not only deer,

Fig. 22. Bow Making (MPM Neg. 500895).

but also animals which prey on the deer. Deer calls are still very common, and easily purchased from the men.

BOWS AND ARROWS. The Kickapoo bow is of the self variety tapering toward either end. The bowstring is of twisted buckskin held in position by end notches in the bow. The best bow wood is imported from Oklahoma. Several men were engaged in bow making during our stay, using hatchet, knife, and glass scraper (Fig. 22). The specimen shown here (Fig. 24) is 44 inches long. Arrows are of several types. The usual hunting arrow is 2 feet or less in length and spirally fletched with either two or three vanes from turkey feathers, bound on with sinew. They are pointed either with tiny, flat, triangular steel heads inserted in the split end and bound with sinew, or with conical steel heads wedged onto the sharpened shaft. Fishing arrows are longer (up to 32 inches) with a conical head, and usually, but not always, without fletching.

The arrow is released by the primary method with the bow being held with the thumb up the back of the bow and the index finger pointing straight forward,

Fig. 23. Arrow Release (MPM Neg. 196146).

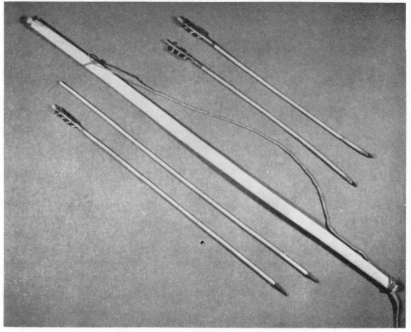

Fig. 24. Bow and Types of Arrows (MPM Neg. 203831).

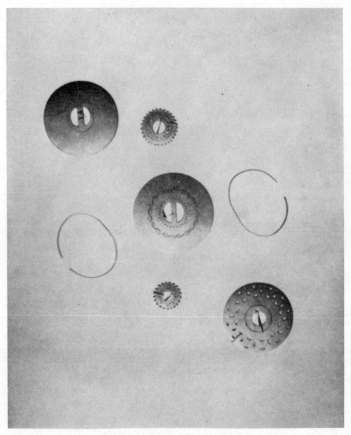

Fig. 25. Silverwork (MPM Neg. 203814).

so that the arrow slides along it (Fig. 23). The rifle has replaced the bow in hunting, but bow and arrows are still used by the men in games, and occasionally for fishing. Among the boys, however, the bow is the most important possession.

Silverwork

Another craft of the men is silverworking. We were informed that there were three silversmiths in the village. We saw some of the products of one of these, but did not have the opportunity of examining his tools. Only German silver (copper, zinc, and nickel) is used, and the products include combs worn by the women at the back of the head, bar brooches, earrings, finger rings, and bracelets (Fig. 25). The articles are made for woman's use, with the exception of neckerchief slides, still in occasional use, and earrings said to have been commonly worn in the pierced earlobes of the men in former times.

One specimen of real silver was obtained, a neckerchief slide purportedly made from a peso, and used as an ornament on a brass-bead necklace (Fig. 26).

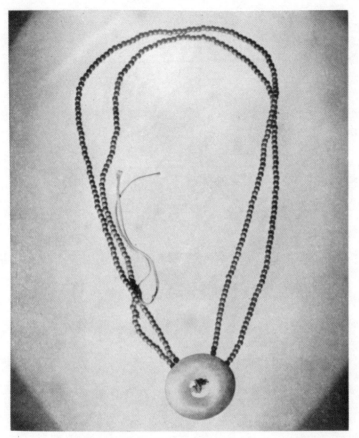

Fig. 26. Brass Necklace with Silver Pendant (MPM Neg. 203801).

An especially fine hour-glass hair ornament (Fig. 27) illustrates the use of brooches sewn on to garments to create a design. Small brooches, ¼ inch in diameter, with two perforations near the top for the passage of thread, are sewn onto a green cloth background to produce a pleasing pattern. A silver band at the constriction of the ornament has a perforation at either side through which is looped a piece of buckskin which serves to bind it onto the doubled-up braid of the wearer. This ornament, 7 inches in height, has sateen streamers of bright green and blue attached to the bottom. Some scholars believe that this type of ornament was derived from the German Palatinate, introduced to the Indians by the Pennsylvania Dutch, and carried to Oklahoma by the Delaware.

Weaving

The weaving of both hard and soft textiles is the work of women. Mats and baskets are the chief products, with yarn bags and sashes unimportant. We saw no fingerweaving in process, and no yarn bags or sashes of the traditional type were offered us for sale. We were told, however, that sashes are worn on cere-

Fig. 27. Hair Ornament (MPM Neg. 203803).

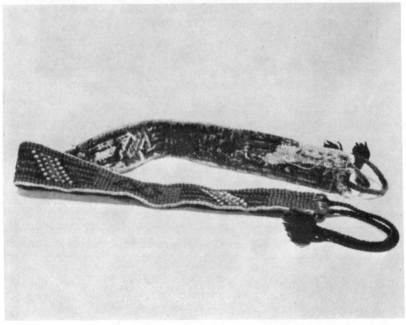

Fig. 28. Modern Yarn Sash (MPM Neg. 203802).

monial occasions, and Goggin (p. 321) illustrates a sash he purchased from them in 1951. We did obtain one unusual yarn sash (Fig. 28). The backing is gunny-cloth embroidered with yarn in geometrical designs. The four braided-yarn ties with tasseled ends illustrate a typical Woodland treatment, but the belt proper is foreign both in weave and design.

Mats are important household articles, being found in considerable number in every house. They are placed along the three sides of the house, often two layers thick, on which they sit, sleep, and eat. The most common type (Fig. 29) is plaited, made of the split elements of sotol leaves, ½ to ¾ inch in width. The elements are left natural or colored with red, blue, green, and yellow commercial dyes, and are incorporated in the mat to produce designs. Although this type of mat is a result of their Mexican experience, they have retained the approximate dimensions of their traditional bulrush mats, 42 to 44 inches wide and about 7 feet long, to conform to the consistent width of the sleeping area of the winter house, and the sleeping platform of the summer house. Such mats can be purchased for about one-third the price.

The bulrush mats of today follow the old Kickapoo weave and designs, although commercial dyes have replaced native varieties, and commercial twine is used for the weft (Fig. 30). They are of excellent weave with attractive patterns and, in our opinion, are the finest craft product of the Mexican Kickapoo.

Fig. 29. Sotol-leaf Mat (MPM Neg. 203812).

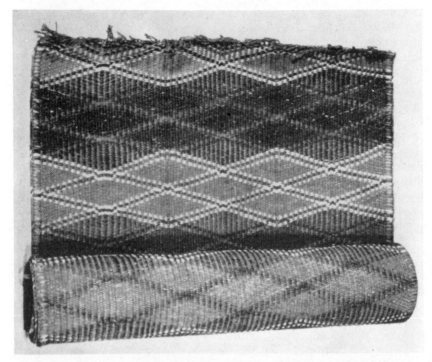

Fig. 30.   Bulrush Mat (MPM Neg. 203800).

A third type of mat, sewn rather than woven, is made of tule stems sewn together with commercial twine by means of steel mat needles, and used for house coverings (Fig. 31). They are undecorated and large in size, averaging about 15 feet in length and 7 feet in width.

Baskets are made in considerable quantity and variety as to size and shape. The bottoms are of plaited sotol leaves, elements of which are bent up to form the sides, into which are twined horizontal strands of dyed bulrush (Fig. 32). A second type incorporates horizontal sotol elements in checkerwork weave, but with alternating horizontal rows formed by double strands of twined bulrush. The majority of these baskets are brightly colored by the use of analine dyes, and equipped with handles. They are made primarily for sale. The Oklahoma Kickapoo do not make baskets of this type, and it is probable that the craft was adopted from the Mexicans.

Leatherwork

Tanning and leatherwork is also the work of women. Buckskin in the process of being tanned is a common sight in the village. The process is similar to that employed by the modern Wisconsin Indians. The hair is removed with a beaming tool consisting of a blade set in a cylindrical piece of wood. The hide is dipped into a solution of dried deer brains and water and thoroughly wrung.

Fig. 31. Tule Mat Making (MPM Negs. 500892, 500891).

Fig. 32. Baskets (MPM Negs. 203811, 203810).

Fig. 33. Buckskin on Drying Frame (MPM Neg. 500866).

It is then laced to a rectangular stretching frame of poles and scraped with a short pole sharpened to an edge at one end (Fig. 33). This process stretches the hide and softens it by breaking down the fibers. When the hide has been stretched and dried, it is taken from the frame, and may be further softened by rubbing it over a staker, a pole set into the ground, equipped with a sharply edged top (Fig. 34). Finally, the hide is suspended over a smudge until it assumes a golden brown color. The tanned hides are used in the making of clothing. Also, some are sold in Muzquiz, and hides are a favorite article of trade with the Oklahoma band.

MOCCASINS. The chief leather product of the Kickapoo today is that of moccasins. They are commonly worn by both men and women, particularly among the middle-aged and older folk. The same style is worn by both sexes, and each moccasin is made of a single piece of buckskin sewn up the heel and toe, and with short cuffs open at front and back and pointed at the front (Fig. 35). A buckskin thong fastened at the front opening is passed under the cuff and around the ankle, and tied in front to hold the moccasin snugly on the foot. Moccasins are commonly decorated with a band of beadwork over the front seam and invariably culminating in a point at the toe end. Beadwork apparently is no longer applied to the cuffs, and no silk-applique decoration, such as is executed by the Oklahoma band, was seen. A feature unique for Woodland folk is the addition of a rawhide

Fig. 34. Fleshing Stake (MPM Neg. 35-16:33).

Fig. 35. Moccasins (MPM Neg. 203804).

Fig. 36. Moccasins with Rawhide Soles (MPM Neg. 35-17:35).

sole on some of the men's moccasins (Fig. 36), apparently an adaptation to the rough hunting trails in the mountains.

LEGGINGS. Leggings (Fig. 37) are rarely worn at present, except during ceremonials and games. The civil chief was the only person observed wearing them for everyday use, and he wore them over a pair of trousers. A legging is made from a single piece of buckskin which is folded lengthwise and sewn up the full length, the seam located about one-third in from the outer edge so as to leave a generous flap. A hidden stitch is used so that the seam is not apparent from the outside. At intervals along and in front of the seam are hung decorative tassels of colored yarn suspended from short lengths of braided buckskin. A strip of buckskin, with the lower half split, and with each split end stitched to the top of the legging near the seam, whereas the upper end is fastened to the belt of the wearer, holds the legging up.

House Types

House building is a cooperative venture by men and women, with the women doing most of the work although the men perform the heavier tasks. The Kickapoo utilize four types of structures during the year: a winter house, summer house, cook hut, and menstrual hut.

The winter house (wikiup, Fig. 38) is the typical Central Algonkian wigwam except for its being covered completely with tule mats instead of having mat sides

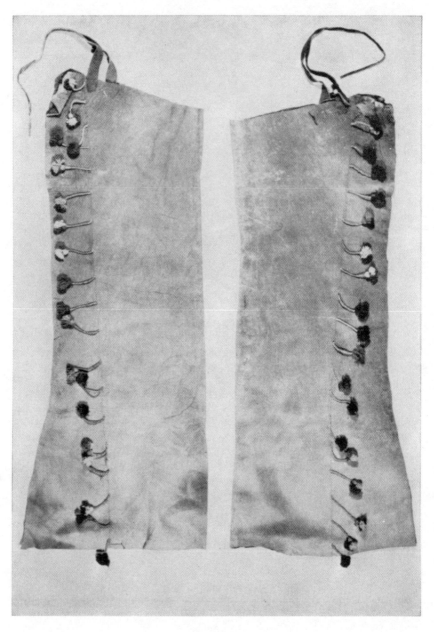

Fig. 37. Leggings (MPM Neg. 203807).

Fig. 38. Winter House (MPM Neg. 35-16:35).

and birch-bark top. It is also larger than that currently seen in Wisconsin, and quite standardized as to size. It is occupied from October to March, after which the mats are transferred to the summer house and the winter framework is dismantled. The wigwam we occupied had a frame consisting of 29 poles, each about 2 inches in diameter at the base, set into the ground to form an ellipse 20 feet in length and 14 feet in width. The poles were bent and tied to form a dome-shaped roof 9 feet in maximum height. Twenty-one poles were tied on horizontally to form a network of rectangles strong enough to utilize as a ladder on which to climb in order to fasten the matting. All binding was done with split sotol leaves. Two openings were left: a doorway (which always faces east) 6 feet high and 1½ feet wide, and a rectangular smokehole 6 feet long and 2 feet wide centrally placed in the roof, but somewhat nearer the front. The roof was strengthened by a sort of ridge pole 9 feet long and 4 inches in diameter, supported by two forked posts set into the floor 7 feet apart. A chain hung from the ridge pole for the suspension of pots over the fire.

The framework was covered with sewn tule mats of double thickness and of a specially large size: about 7 by 15 feet in cross dimensions. The mats were bound onto the framework so that the tule stems were disposed up and down, and one mat overlapped another, so that the end result was a shelter which kept out wind and rain quite effectively. The doorway was covered with a canvas flap. Most wikiups also have a slat door which opens to the inside.

In cold weather the wikiup can be kept reasonably warm with a wood fire, although it is not the most efficient heating arrangement as most of the heat

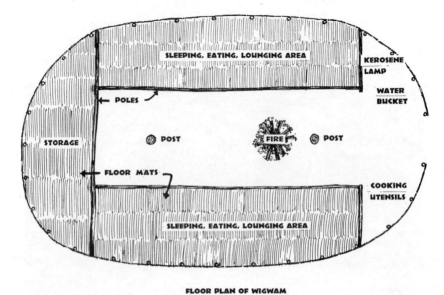

FLOOR PLAN OF WIGWAM

Fig. 39. Wikiup Floor Plan.

Fig. 40. Summer House (MPM Neg. 500886-B).

Fig. 41. Summer House Framework (MPM Neg. 35-16:1).

Fig. 42. Wall Detail of Summer House (MPM Neg. 35-17:30).

Fig. 43. Summer House Interior (MPM Neg. 500858).

goes out of the smoke hole. The floor plan of a wikiup is shown in figure 39.

The summer house (odanikani, Fig. 40) is occupied from March to October. Unlike the wikiup, the framework of the summer house (Fig. 41) can be left standing for as long as four years before a new one must be built. When the village decides to change quarters, the mats from the wikiup are transferred to the roof of the summer house, after any necessary repairs to the framework and mats have been made, and after cleaning up the interior. The framework of the wikiup is then torn down. The summer house always faces east, and each has a ramada or sun shelter adjoining the front. The summer house in our compound was 18 feet square, with cane walls 6 feet in height. The "cane" was actually sotol flower stalks which are about 1½ inches in diameter and fairly rigid. They were bound on to the pole framework in pairs, leaving generous gaps between (Fig. 42). The pole framework serving as roof structure sloped downward on all four sides from a rounded peak, in this instance 11 feet high. A ridgepole, similar in size and manner of suspension to that in the wikiup, spanned the apex roof of the framework. A smoke hole was left, comparable in size and position to that in the wikiup.

The interior differs from that of the wikiup in one respect: the mats, instead of resting on the floor, are placed on sleeping platforms constructed along the two sides and back (Fig. 43). In the house that we measured, these racks were

Fig. 44. Cook and Storage Hut (MPM Neg. 35-17:29).

5 feet wide and 2 feet 4 inches high. Each was supported by six crotched posts set into the ground three on each side to hold poles, across which were bound cross sticks. Sotol stalks were laid lengthwise on top and tied to the cross pieces, and a layer or two of mats made the platform usable for sleeping or lounging.

In front of each summer house is a ramada consisting of a rounded roof supported by poles set into the ground. The roof is a few feet lower than that of the summer house, and its pole framework is covered with either brush or tule mats. Racks of similar construction to those in the summer house extend along the two sides, serving as seats in the daytime and beds at night when the weather is hot. No cooking is done in the ramada.

A third type of structure in the Kickapoo compound is represented by the cook and storage huts (Fig. 44). These are of similar construction to the summer house but are smaller and not as well built, and do not have to face east. The one in our compound was 11 feet square. A storage rack 3 feet wide bordered the rear wall, and a chain hung from the ridgepole from which pots could be suspended over the fire. These huts are used for the storage of food, and for cooking the meals during the hot summer months.

The fourth type of structure, the menstrual hut (Fig. 45), is placed at one corner of the compound with no special orientation. These are small, nondescript, temporary-looking huts, some resembling a tiny wikiup, others a small cook hut. The roof is usually covered with brush or tattered canvas, and the only opening

Fig. 45. Menstrual Hut (MPM Neg. 35-15:13).

is a doorway. Food is brought to the menstruating woman, who must eat and sleep alone in the hut during this period, when she is considered to have a contaminating effect on all with which she comes in contact. For her to touch the food of others, for example, could cause illness and even death.

While this discussion of Kickapoo material culture is based on limited field observations and a small sample of their products, it does, nevertheless, cover the range of their arts and crafts. Besides the specimens in the Milwaukee Public Museum, there are collections of Mexican Kickapoo materials at the Chicago Museum of Natural History, and the National Museum in Mexico City.

BIBLIOGRAPHY

Fabila, Alfonso.*
  1945. La Tribu Kickapoo de Coahuila. Biblioteca Enciclopedica Popular,
        No. 50. Mexico.

Goggin, John M.
  1951. The Mexican Kickapoo Indians. Southwestern Jr. of Anthrop., Vol.
        7, No. 3.

Harrington, M. R.
  1944. Too Much Hominy. The Masterkey, Vol. 18, No. 5, pp. 155-6.

Jones, William.
  1939. Ethnography of the Fox Indians. B.A.E. Bull. 125.

Mexican Govt.
  . . . . . Archivos, Oficina de Colonizacion, Secretaria de Agricultura y Fo-
        mento. Book 74, Sheaf #3, 16th Item. Mexico City.
  1875. Report of the Committee of Investigation, sent in 1873 by the Gov-
        ernment to the Frontier of Texas, translated from the Official Mexi-
        can Edition. Baker & Godwin, New York.

Michelson, Truman.
  1927. Notes on the Ceremonial Runners of the Fox Indians. B.A.E. Bull.
        85.

Mooney, James and Jones, William.
  1907. Kickapoo. B.A.E. Bull. 30, Vol. 1, pp. 684-5.

Porter, Kennth.
  1952. The Seminole-Negro-Indian Scouts, 1870-1881. Southwest Histor.
        Quart., Vol. 55, No. 3.

Silverberg, J.
  1949. The Cultural Position of the Kickapoo. M. A. Thesis, University of
        Wisconsin. Madison, Wis.

Tax, Sol.
  1937. The Social Organization of the Fox Indians. In Social Anthropology
        of the North American Indian Tribes, Eggan, F. (Ed.), University
        of Chicago Press.

U. S. Senate.
  1908. Affairs of the Mexican Kickapoo Indians. Senate Document 215,
        parts 1-3, 60th Congress, 1st Session. Washington.

---

* The material in this booklet is reported to have been obtained and written by Mr. Enrique Gallan Long
whose manuscript was published under the name of Fabila.